American Society

Tool Kit Included

Training Design and Delivery

A single-source guide for every trainer, training manager, and occasional trainer

Geri E. McArdle

Ordering information: Books published by the American Society for Training & Development can be ordered by calling 800.628.2783 or 703.683.8100.

Library of Congress Catalog Card Number: 98-68521
ISBN: 1-56286-099-2

Contents

Preface

Training is an industry. In the past 15 years, the field of training and professional development has grown enormously. In the United States, it is estimated that yearly corporations spend $60 billion on training employees, but statistics indicate that very little of that investment is returned to the workplace.

Management offers skill and education and professional development training, hoping that it will increase personal and workplace satisfaction, motivation, and productivity, but the return-on-investment can be realized only if training programs, both informal and formal, are well defined, delivered, and evaluated.

Training Design and Delivery provides a comprehensive resource for training managers and trainers who are responsible for the planning, organization, design, implementation, and evaluation of training programs. The principles in this book can serve as a tutorial for new and developing trainers. Managers who have to develop and deliver a training program will also find this book of value.

The book consists of two parts. The first part opens with a training systems model, which is a theoretical model that establishes the theory, or set of facts, which provides a focus for organizing the topics. This model describes a 20-step process for analyzing, designing, developing, implementing, and evaluating training interventions.

The second part is a trainer's tool kit, which provides answers to the major problem areas you may encounter during design and implementation. The tool kit itself has two sections. The first describes the technique, and the second, the application of each technique.

Training Design and Delivery is applicable to training in almost every sector: commercial, industrial, as well as in universities and colleges and organizations in the public and private sectors.

I wrote this book with myself in mind. When I began my career as a trainer and human resource manager, I couldn't find a simple book that described the steps to use in developing and implementing training. I promised myself that once I'd mastered the process, I would share it with others so they wouldn't have the fear of the unknown that I had without a road map.

This book is your personal road map to training success.

Geri E. McArdle
Reston, Virginia
February 1999

Introduction

These are exciting times. With advances in computer technology, we're all witnessing a revitalized effort in the fields of knowledge engineering, expert systems, and multimedia educational technology. For many people, these emerging technologies are tools in training design and delivery systems and in the way we study learning and conceive of the learning process.

My own discovery of instructional systems design (ISD) in industry and the current movement toward performance systems technology have an impact on my role and responsibility as a trainer and an instructional designer. Training interventions must consist of a well planned, organized learning event that can ensure an outcome for the learning and for the sponsoring organization. I'm sure you, too, have encountered or are starting to encounter ripples from these trends in designing and delivering training that provide a return on both investment training dollars and the use of cutting-edge technology.

No matter how high-tech or low-tech you and your training designs may be, they will have to adhere to the demanding standards of training design. No training intervention is successful unless the instructional design meets these standards of quality, and that quality of design, development, and delivery has its basis in a scientific approach in the area of human learning.

MULTISTEP MODEL

This book provides a multistep training program that is an easy-to-use guide for designing and developing a training module and program, whether it will be a computerized program or a low-tech, in-house workshop. The steps take the reader from responding to the initial training request to delivering and evaluating the training program. Specifically created for this book, the model sets forth a number of critical elements. Although hundreds of training practitioners use the critical elements in this model when they design and develop training programs, the model organizes them and begins with a little-used step, business justification. This first step—business justification—leads management to buy into the training intervention, which is essential for successful training.

By following the training system model, you will be on the road to providing successful training interventions.

Defining the Purpose

The purpose of establishing a training system in an organization is to ensure you design programs that

- respond to the organization's business needs
- are educationally sound
- produce learning that is measurable.

USING A TRAINING SYSTEM MODEL

You can use the training system model (see figure 1) as a guideline for developing new training programs or revising existing training programs.

The six-stage model—business justification, needs assessment, design, development, implementation, and evaluation—follows a systems approach to planning, preparing, conducting, and evaluating training programs. Each stage involves specific techniques from the field of instructional technology. For example, the information you obtain through a needs analysis becomes the starting point for obtaining job analysis data. Then you use the information you obtain from the job analysis to determine the instructional objectives.

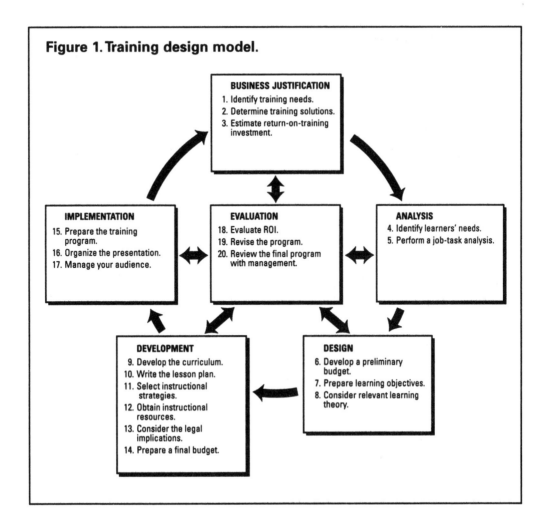

Figure 1. Training design model.

BUSINESS JUSTIFICATION
1. Identify training needs.
2. Determine training solutions.
3. Estimate return-on-training investment.

IMPLEMENTATION
15. Prepare the training program.
16. Organize the presentation.
17. Manage your audience.

EVALUATION
18. Evaluate ROI.
19. Revise the program.
20. Review the final program with management.

ANALYSIS
4. Identify learners' needs.
5. Perform a job-task analysis.

DEVELOPMENT
9. Develop the curriculum.
10. Write the lesson plan.
11. Select instructional strategies.
12. Obtain instructional resources.
13. Consider the legal implications.
14. Prepare a final budget.

DESIGN
6. Develop a preliminary budget.
7. Prepare learning objectives.
8. Consider relevant learning theory.

DETERMINING THE RATIONALE

The model addresses three questions critical to any training program developer:

- What content should I include?
- How should I teach and deliver the content?
- How can I ensure that the training is working (that is, that trainees learn the content)?

STEPS OF THE TRAINING SYSTEM MODEL

The training system model has a total of 20 steps. The steps in the business justification stage, chapter 2, are as follows:

1. Identify training needs. Conduct a preliminary needs analysis. Determine what kind of performance problems the organization is experiencing. Find out who thinks these are problems and why. Use observation, questionnaires, interviews, tests, work samples, and records to help identify the training need.

2. Determine training solutions. Training does not solve all performance problems, and it is important to determine that training will solve the problem that management believes exists. Thorough analysis of the needs will help to determine if training is the solution to the performance deficiencies.

3. Estimate return-on-investment (ROI). The process of measuring ROI should be simple, economical, and credible as well as theoretically sound, flexible, and applicable with all types of data, including hard data such as output, quality, costs, and time and soft data such as job satisfaction, customer satisfaction, grievances, and complaints.

Analysis, chapter 3, has two steps:

4. Identify learners' needs. Collect data on the needs of individuals who are or will be performing the tasks. Production records, performance appraisals, supervisors, and the employees can provide the information needed to identify learners' needs.

5. Perform a so-called job-task analysis. Once it is determined that training will solve the performance problems, analyze all the tasks that make up performance for particular jobs.

The following steps are in the design stage, chapter 4:

6. Develop a preliminary budget. Estimate the costs to decide whether to design or buy a training program.

7. Prepare learning objectives. Objectives, which are specific statements of what learners will do or know upon completion of the training, help define the content of the training program and

ensure that the tasks required to perform are included in the program. Decide to create or buy a program.

8. Consider relevant learning theory. Different theories explain how people learn, which occurs internally and at best can be inferred.

The development stage, chapter 5, has the following steps:

9. Develop the curriculum. The written documents should reflect the interaction of content, sequence, instructor's experience, learners' experience, and organization's expectations.

10. Write the lesson plan. Include in the plan the learning objective, content, instructor and learner activities, test items, and enabling knowledge.

11. Select instructional strategies. Strategies range from audiovisual equipment to a variety of group learning techniques. The lesson plan may need to be revised after selecting instructional strategies.

12. Obtain instructional resources. After completing the first draft of the training program, designers must make plans for the physical, financial, and human resources needed to conduct the program.

13. Consider the legal implications. Before pursuing the training in earnest, designers must check for possible violations of the law that the training program might create. These include copyright infringement and equal employment opportunity laws.

14. Prepare the final budget. The final budget is a complete estimate of training costs that is presented to management.

Implementation, chapter 6, has these three steps:

15. Prepare the training program. During this step, you organize the content of the learning module. You learn about the audience and venue, and select the materials and format.

16. Organize the presentation. Plan the meat of your presentation, choosing to follow the theory or skill session model, and writing the body, conclusion, and introduction. You select the method of delivery, including the visual aids you'll use.

17. Manage your audience. Watch their reactions and gauge their interest as you speak. Modify your presentation to be sure they remain in tune with you.

The final stage, evaluation, has the following steps:

18. Evaluate the results of training and return-on-investment to the organizational operations. Has the training improved performance such that the organization's overall economic picture has improved? Measures such as sales and absenteeism can be tied to training.

19. Revise the program. Throughout the training program it is important to obtain feedback and to refine the program to best meet the learners' and organization's needs.

20. Review the final program with appropriate levels of management. Various levels of management participate in reviewing the final training program. Management support must follow through well after learners complete the training program to ensure that the training had the desired results.

With full knowledge of the benefits and elements of training, it is important to convince management about how training will affect the organization's economic picture. The next chapter presents information about developing a business justification for training.

Although each chapter is self-contained and is designed to provide specific skills and techniques, as dictated by the 20-step ISD model that forms the road map for this book, in practice a number of questions and needs do arise with the development of a training intervention. The tool kit provides tools and techniques that respond to the most often asked questions and to frequent tool needs. A quick review of the tool kit now can add real competence to your real-life practice.

▬Business Justification

The first step in designing a training program is to determine the business justification behind the training request and the implications of conducting, or not conducting, the training program. Managers use results of the business justification to:

- decide whether to provide the training
- allocate resources
- prioritize a training program for scheduling purposes.

Businesses, business units, organizations, and associations all are concerned with leadership and motivation, though to different degrees. To best appeal to businesses that think that training will solve a performance problem, trainers should embody the following leadership qualities:

- Set a good example.
- Seek and take on new challenges.
- Be courageous in facing the unknown.
- Demonstrate resourcefulness when confronting and solving problems.
- Show concern for trainees' and organizations' well-being and success.

The ultimate criterion of leadership is the ability to inspire these same qualities in others to motivate changes in their behavior directed toward achieving specific goals. Trainers who demonstrate leadership traits are attractive to management. Businesses look for these kinds of qualities in their employees. Presenting yourself as a leader is a key element behind business justification for training.

Let's carry the importance of leadership to business justification a bit further. Leadership, although an abstraction, can be recognized in others. People can learn leadership by using others as role models and by attending effective training programs. As a trainer, you more than likely will be asked to develop a training program that solves a performance gap. The training you give to fill that gap should embody characteristics of leadership. By incorporating leadership qualities, you provide an environment in which employees are motivated to take on the challenge of applying what they learn.

If employees emerge from training with a sense that through the training the organization has sought to increase their well-being, the employees are likely to feel more committed to the organization's well-being. This return to the organization is definitely a business justification for training.

Employees can be confident about their abilities to perform on the job without being motivated to improve their performance. A properly designed and implemented training program will instill confidence and motivation in the people you train. Training that is based on a specific context and on techniques specific to the workplace will demonstrate that change is not only possible but also desirable, and, thus, will be a further step in motivating employees to change.

As a trainer, you can help the organization determine if a business justification for the training exists by conducting performance and business analyses.

CONDUCTING A PERFORMANCE ANALYSIS

A performance analysis is a process for determining if a training need or opportunity exists. During the course of a performance analysis, you must answer the following questions:

- Who is the client?
- What is the problem or the need?

- What are the reasons for the problem or need?
- Why is the request being made now?
- What performance enhancement or deficiency is the training intended to address?
- What is the value or worth of the problem or need?
- Are there any red flags (for example, internal politics) that you need to consider?
- Who is the target population?
- What are the alternative ways in which the problem or need could be addressed?

Present the performance analysis summary containing the following information as a written report or as an oral presentation:

- need or needs identification
- reason or reasons the need arose
- value or worth of the need or cost of not addressing it
- alternative actions available to address the need
- description of the target population
- explanation of how training can address the need
- description of the client's training objectives
- overview of tasks, skills, or knowledge, or combination of them, to be covered
- red flags or other training concerns to be considered.

CONDUCTING A BUSINESS ANALYSIS

A business analysis is a process for determining the return to the organization of investing in the training program. The business analysis should address the following questions:

- What consequences will the training have on the organization's performance?
- Why is training perceived to be the solution?
- What are the clients' training objectives?

- What tasks, skills, or knowledge, or combination, will the training program content cover?
- What alternative ways could the organization address the training problem or need?
- How would each of the alternatives enhance the organization's business strategy?
- How much does each alternative cost (in total resources required)?
- Which is the preferred alternative (with rationale)?
- What is the anticipated level of client commitment?
- What roles and responsibilities will each member of the training project team have?
- Are the required resources available from within the organization?
- Are the required resources available from outside the organization?
- Are there any constraints that will affect planning, preparing, and conducting this training program?
- Are there any nontraining issues that might affect the program's progress?

Present the business analysis summary as a written report or as an oral presentation. It should cover the following issues:

- implications for the organization
- what the consequence would be on the organization's performance if the training were conducted or were not conducted
- alternative methods by which the training department can meet the training need
- costs of each alternative
- how each alternative might enhance the organization's business strategy
- preferred alternative, with rationale
- organization-related constraints affecting the training program's design, development, or delivery
- client-related constraints affecting the training program's design or development, or both

- implications for the training unit
- anticipated level of client commitment and support
- roles and responsibilities of all training program team members
- resources required and their availability
- nontraining issues that might affect the training program's progress.

You should draw your recommendations and conclusions from the performance and business analyses.

PREPARING THE TRAINING PROJECT AGREEMENT

The final aspect of the business justification involves preparing a brief training project agreement, as shown in figure 1. The purpose of the agreement is to ensure that the client understands exactly what training program will be provided.

The training project agreement should accomplish the following:

- describe the training program
- define preliminary objectives
- provide timelines for project completion
- list resources required
- identify any program limitations or constraints.

Budget allocations should be made after all the parties involved have signed the agreement.

Each of the following chapters covers one of the next five steps in the training system model:

- analysis
- design
- development
- implementation
- evaluation.

Figure 1. A brief training project agreement outlines components of the program.

TRAINING PROJECT AGREEMENT

Project Name _____

Project Manager _____

Client Project Manager _____

Sponsor _____

OVERVIEW

Description of Training Project _____

_____

_____

Description of Preliminary Objectives _____

_____

_____

WORK PLAN

Project Start_____ Printer Materials Review _____ Pilot Test _____

Course Outline Review_____ Dry Run/Test_____ Course Release _____

Internal Resources Required (Who? When?) _____

_____

External Resources Required _____

Limitation or Constraints_____

_____

Sales Guide and Software Availability_____

_____

Assumptions and Contingencies _____

_____

_____ _____ _____
Project Manager   Sponsor   Client

_____ _____ _____
Date   Date   Date

3

Analysis

INTRODUCTION

After completing the business justification and obtaining a signed training project agreement, you are ready to begin the second stage of the training system model, a needs analysis, also called a needs assessment. Briefly, needs analysis is a systematic process of discovery to support change through training or retraining. Needs analysis is the second step in the training system model because the information collected (using a combination of needs analysis tools) enables you to define specifically the gaps between current and desired organizational and individual performance. During the needs analysis process, you will identify problems or other issues to determine if there is a need for training and if training is the appropriate intervention.

This phase gives you the opportunity to examine the context of a particular job, the skills required for performing the job, and the on-the-job knowledge required before you deliver any training intervention. An error at this second stage can throw off the entire training process and usually results in an unsuccessful training program. To guarantee successful design and implementation of training, be sure to include the following:

- Define the trainer's role.
- Follow the six strategies to guarantee success.

- Identify the learners' needs.
- Complete the four-step needs analysis process.

OVERVIEW OF THE NEEDS ANALYSIS

Define the Trainer's Role

As a trainer, you have a unique opportunity to interact with everyone in your organization because your role provides you with access to everyone in the organization. There exist no artificial barriers or concerns about authority. The trainer serves everyone in the organization, and, therefore, has unspoken permission to gain access to all levels within the organization.

When gathering data and delivering training, a trainer is like a detective sifting through information and analyzing it to determine if there are problems and what the evidence is for them.

Follow the Six Strategies to Guarantee Success

Although organizations operate differently and training varies with jobs and tasks, research shows that successful training initiatives have common features, which include the following:

1. *Management commitment:* Involving management early in the needs analysis process benefits everyone. Management is often the driving force behind a needs analysis. Remember that management requests training. You must have management's support before beginning an analysis. The training project agreement described in chapter two represents such support. By conducting a needs analysis in an environment that fosters mutual respect and honesty, you give yourself every advantage for reaching an agreement with management about the outcome of the analysis.

2. *Rationale for training intervention:* It will save time and money to determine if training is an appropriate intervention. Providing a training intervention simply because management requests or requires it does not guarantee success. You must decide if the issue under discussion calls for training. You must also establish the following:

- how the proposed training affects the proposed audience
- acceptance from the likely audience, supervisors, and management
- training's effect on the entire organization.

3. *Questions that guide the process:* Defining the problem clearly is critical to developing a successful training intervention. Answers to the following two questions help define the area of need:
   - Why is it that people do or don't perform?
   - What performance is desired?

4. *Factors that influence the process:* It is important to examine knowledge, skills, and attitudes in the analysis. The work environment is an important factor in the process. So, too, is examining in detail individuals' skills, knowledge, and attitudes about their tasks, jobs, boss, and the organization. Together, these factors influence your decision about whether to provide a training intervention. They show that the problem has to do with an environmental problem (poor lighting, for example) or that it is the result of unrealistic deadlines, not inefficient training.

5. *Types of intervention:* It is important to differentiate between the two types of intervention:
   - training, which teaches an immediate job skill
   - education, which provides theories, content, and knowledge to be applied in the future.

6. *Performance standards and criteria:* Establishing standards of excellence and using them as performance criteria are basic to operating an organization. Use the following three indicators to measure individual and organizational performance:
   - What should and does the organization consider baseline skills?
   - What is the group intelligence of the individuals, groups, departments, and organization?
   - What behaviors and attitudes exist?

Identify the Learners' Needs

Learners' needs, which in general relate to performance, can be divided into two classes—micro and macro. A micro need is one that exists for one person or for a very small population. A macro need is one that exists for a large group of employees, frequently for the entire population with the same job classifications. You must consider both types of needs during the analysis stage. Some typical micro needs are (Laird, 1985):

- New employees need to understand what is expected on the job.
- A three-person unit is expected to know how to operate newly installed microcomputers.
- A supervisor is having problems managing his or her time.

Examples of macro needs are as follows:

- All employees need orientation when the company opens a new building.
- All employees are expected to be able to use a newly installed, companywide computer system.
- All first-line supervisors are required to initiate performance appraisal discussions in their units.

Complete the Four-Step Needs Analysis Process

The following four steps will help ensure a successful outcome when conducting your analysis: surveillance, investigation, analysis, and reporting.

Step One: Surveillance

Scan the organization to determine if there is an organizational need or a performance gap. In completing this step, you will check the details of management's request to ensure that it is a training need.

Define the need and identify any performance gaps. A complete definition of the identified performance gaps ensure that neither time nor money will be wasted pursuing an end that won't solve the problems. Using analytical tools you can focus on clearly defining the problem. Training is meant to effect a change in behavior. To bring about any such change, you must first identify a performance gap.

During surveillance you will determine if a training intervention is appropriate. To make that determination, you must gather sufficient information, define the kind of information you need, determine where to obtain it, and gain access to it. Answers to the following six questions will determine the nature of the problem:

1. Why this issue?
2. Whose need is it, and who is involved?
3. What is the issue?
4. When did this issue become a need?
5. Where did the issue begin?
6. What is the best way to solve this issue?

Meet with the client. The goal of this meeting is to determine specific factors to be analyzed and the type and level of support you can expect throughout the analysis and training design process. Two parts are involved: defining premeeting issues and managing the meeting.

- Premeeting
    — Contact client and schedule meeting.
    — Identify other staff, if any, who should attend.
    — Prepare a questionnaire to record data.
    — Explain next steps in the process.

- Meeting
    — Define the task.
    — Agree on need and training outcome.
    — Establish shared responsibility and identify a contact person for the report.
    — Obtain commitment to proceed.

Before the first meeting, you will need to complete a premeeting guide, which is shown in figure 1. Then, at the first meeting, you will want to obtain responses to the issues about the target task, participants, and training session identified in a meeting guide, which appears in figure 2.

Next, write the client a summary memo as soon as possible after the initial client meeting. The memo should request a written commitment to continue the needs analysis, state agreed-upon allocation of resources and training outcomes, and establish a project timeline that outlines all the steps in the needs analysis process. Figure 3 is an example of a client summary memorandum.

Figure 1. Example of a premeeting guide.

NEEDS ASSESSMENT CLIENT MEETING #1: PREMEETING INFORMATION

Date: _____

Place: _____

Time: _____

Contact: _____

Position: _____

Training issue(s): _____

_____

Guiding questions or topics: _____

_____

Next steps: _____

_____

Finally, identify key data sources. Now you are ready to decide what information to collect, which audience to survey, and which tools to use to collect and analyze the data. There are two kinds of data: hard and soft. Hard data are the factual and objective information that comes from reports and accounting records. Soft data are opinions and other subjective information that come from group discussions, interviews, and questionnaires. Table 1 shows the advantages and disadvantages of key hard data sources.

Step Two: Investigation

Once you have gathered your information in step one, you should organize it, review your initial information, and determine the type of data to determine your next step in designing a training intervention. Now you can select the data-collection method you will use and can begin gathering further data that will permit you to make some assumptions about the issues and create some alternatives for resolving the problem.

During the investigation, you are conducting research to determine whether a lack of training or some other organizational deficiency is causing the performance problem. Use the following questions to help establish some investigative parameters:

Figure 2. Example of a meeting guide.

NEEDS ASSESSMENT CLIENT MEETING #1: MEETING GUIDELINES	
About the target task	**Responses**
Organization's performance standards	
Work conditions	
Supervisor's performance expectations	
About the participants	**Responses**
Stated training need(s)	
Current performance level(s)	
Current level(s) of knowledge	
Attitudes toward task	
Attitudes toward training	
About the training session	**Responses**
Timeframe for planning	
Stakeholders	
Conditions under which training will be conducted	
Available resources (e.g., materials, tools)	
Instructor's skills	

> **Figure 3. Example of a client summary memorandum.**
>
> **MEMORANDUM**
>
> **To:** Client
> **From:** Trainer or facilitator
> **Date:** January 2, 1999
> **Subject:** Needs assessment client meeting
>
> 1. Statement of the Problem
>   Write a clear statement describing the assessment and training outcomes mutually agreed upon during the meeting.
> 2. Description of Tasks
>   Define the task you perceived to be involved in the needs assessment process.
> 3. Summary of Analyses
>   Summarize the information about the target tasks, the participants, and the training situation that would be informative to help management make a commitment to the process and the proposed training outcome.
> 4. Proposed Plan
>   Present your plan for conducting the assessment including tasks, timeline, and a project budget.
> 5. Request for Management's Commitment
>   Request the client's written commitment to the project.

- What results does the organization obtain?
- How do these results compare with the organization's key objectives?
- What contribution does the training department need to make to meet the organization's key objectives?
- What method or methods do you currently use to set priorities and justify training targets?
- How do you measure training results?

Data Collection. The problem or problems to be addressed will guide your method for collecting data and the type of data you will collect. You should select from questionnaires, interviews (one-on-one, telephone, or focus groups), observations, precourse assignments, documentation, job descriptions, and policies and procedures.

Table 1. Comparison of key hard data sources.			
METHOD	**DESCRIPTION**	**ADVANTAGE**	**DISADVANTAGE**
Human resource records	Provide causes regarding performance problems and training issues	Objective	Time-consuming
Accident and safety reports	Reveal clusters of issue types by department and position	Quantitative	Does not necessarily document causes
Grievance filings and turnover rates	State problem with employee or immediate supervisor	Documentation	Issues may be related to policy rather than to training
Performance evaluation and merit ratings	Measured analysis of employees on absolute and relative bases	Documents skills and employee progress	Subjective infor-mation
Production statistics	Numerical results of out-put and itemized costs of doing business	Quantitative	Does not always provide a complete picture

As you collect data, remember that before solving any problem, you must clearly define the situation. Some tips for doing so follow:

- Ask who, what, why, when, and how questions.
- Develop a clear and concise problem statement.
- Separate facts from opinions.
- Document causes of the problem.
- Identify feelings about the problem.
- Determine who is involved and why.
- Formulate a resolution based on facts.

Obtain management's buy-in to proceed. Make sure you have received a written response to paragraph 5 of the client summary memorandum (figure 3) requesting management's commitment to the project.

The commitment letter in figure 4 provides an example of possible wording.

Figure 4. Example of a client commitment letter.

XYZ Company
1000 The Street
City, State, Zip Code
Area Code Phone Number

February 2, 1999

Ms. Dew Wright
Human Resources Director
XYZ Company
1234 The Street
City, State, Zip Code

Dear Ms. Wright:

As president of XYZ Company, I hereby fully support the project's objectives and proposed training outcomes, as stated in your January 25 summary memorandum. Concomitant with this commitment is the agreed upon availability of resources as requested.

With all best wishes for success, I remain,

Sincerely yours,

Philip Phillips
President

Determine skills, knowledge, and attitudes. In some circumstances, the issue that management identified may not be a training problem. So as not to waste training time, money, and other resources, you need to determine skills, knowledge, and attitudes (SKAs) to determine if they relate to a training problem.

It is critical to investigate SKAs as you conduct your needs analysis. Explore the following factors that cause performance problems:

- *Lack of skills and knowledge to do the job:* Can employees do the job tasks needed to meet the performance goals? If the answer is yes, there is no training problem and some other intervention should be considered.

- *Lack of specific standards or job expectations:* Do employees know and understand their performance expectations?
- *Lack of feedback:* Do employees receive feedback about their performance?
- *Lack of necessary resources to perform:* Do employees have everything they need to perform?
- *Lack of appropriate consequences for performance:* Do employees receive appropriate incentives to perform adequately?

The recommendation for solving the problem may comprise several solutions, often involving training and some organizational intervention. When a training deficit exists, further analysis is needed to determine the scope of a training intervention. At this point, you will usually conduct audience and job analyses, using analysis profiles like the completed forms in tables 2 and 3. You would complete table 2 through interviews with people who want training conducted to acquire a narrative of the people who are likely to need the training. You may conduct several pretraining interviews for one program, speaking with several supervisors and potential participants, for example. You may then complete several audience profiles, according to the number of people you interview, which you would then integrate into one form. There are four factors to consider when analyzing your training audience: education, work experience, previous training, and implementation. On the basis of your analysis of table 2, you may propose that the training manager and finance manager attend a one-day train-the-trainer workshop.

For table 3, you would have a conversational interview with people doing the job as well as with supervisors. The profile forms the structure of the interview. The results of the two forms will help you make choices about the language, course material, instructor, and location you will use.

A job analysis is to determine where the training issue really exists. Jobs consist of major functional areas, typically three or four. The job of senior acquisitions editor in book publishing, for example, has three main functions: to identify people who might become authors of books, to coordinate the production of manuscripts, and to conduct book sales at trade shows. Under each of the areas are tasks. The function of coordinating

Table 2. Sample audience analysis profile.

AREA	QUESTIONS	FINDINGS
EDUCATION	Range of school experience	*High school*
	Native language	*English*
	Average reading level	*10th grade*
WORK EXPERIENCE	Existing skills or knowledge related to proposed training	*Basic principles*
	Variation of work experience levels	*1–10 years in finance*
TRAINING	Motivation	*High*
	Recent training experience	*Basic introductory course*
	Effect on current job	*Minimal to concern*
	Degree of accountability	*High: mistakes are easily identified at closing audit*
DELIVERY	Number of people to be trained	*T=30 in 3 districts*
	Location of people to be trained	*Three districts: New York, Maryland, Ohio*

manuscript production, for example, includes preparation of manuscripts for production, which itself includes checking for a copy editor's comments and coordinating those comments with an author's responses.

In conducting a job analysis, trainers must identify enabling knowledge as well as functional areas, tasks, and performance elements. The enabling knowledge for acquisitions editors who coordinate editors' com-

Table 3. Sample job analysis profile.	

JOB TITLE OF TRAINING: _____

FUNCTIONAL RESPONSIBILITIES	TASKS INVOLVED IN EACH
Write 30-minute training module.	Define objectives. Develop topical outline. Decide on instructional strategies. Produce course works.
Evaluate 30-minute training.	Determine level of education. Include test items in design. Determine methods of data collection, analysis, and report.

ments with authors' responses is an understanding of the editor's terminology. A job analysis that breaks down the areas of a job assists trainers and course designers who are trying to determine a training need, say for editors, so they won't subject them to trying on everything about their job.

One of your major responsibilities is to compile on an ongoing basis a list of needs and ideas for training activities. Ideas for the list may come from several channels (for example, a formal needs analysis, a request from a specific unit, a request for training on some newly installed equipment, company literature, and observation of industry trends).

When collecting data, it is helpful to keep an annotated list of the material you keep in your files so you can readily respond to questions about potential training needs. The list also can help you monitor each issue to see where training is necessary. Table 4 shows an annotated list of files. The column on the left specifies the training issue, the middle column describes the current situation, and the column on the right describes the ideal situation. This form is one way to organize information that comes to you through memorandums, newsletters, and other reports.

Continually add data and information to your list of files. By storing information and related data in this master file system or list whenever a training or performance issue arises, you will have some background information on a particular issue.

Table 4. Sample list of files.

AREA	WHAT IS HAPPENING?	WHAT SHOULD BE HAPPENING?
Organization's mission and objectives • Performance standards • Budget targets • Job descriptions • Production • Performance appraisals	*Increase 10% market share in sale of product B. Product has a systems bug.*	*Product B should be leader in industry. Fix, test, and train. Track customer sales.*
Rate of: • Labor turnover • Absenteeism • Accidents • Disciplinary actions	*Behind in midyear appraisal by some management staff.*	*All employees should have review by April each year.*
Costs: • Labor • Materials • Overtime • Economic predictions • Technical development • Legal issues	*Sexual harassment issues. Unknown to staff. Write guidelines. Be specific.*	*Provide latest update from Supreme Court ruling, July 1998.*

When a performance problem exists or an organizational need surfaces, the first thought that pops into people's heads is to train the problem away. However, interventions other than training should be considered. Before thinking about the type of training program, remember that you must determine if training is the appropriate intervention.

If you think a training intervention is needed, use the audience analysis profile in table 2 and the problem analysis profile in figure 5 to establish the need for a training intervention and to help you develop the content. You would observe, interview, and analyze employees with the same or similar jobs and would integrate your findings into one form. This would help you to see where a problem lies, how big it is, whether employees have the skills, and who owns the problem. Without collecting and organizing these data, you would find it difficult to match your training to the participants' needs.

Figure 5. Sample problem analysis profile.

PERFORMANCE AREA _Accounts receivable_

PERFORMANCE GOAL _All reps should exhibit proficiency. Use upgrades for coding billings._

CURRENT PERFORMANCE _30% staff exhibit appropriate competency; 50% to be trained and tested._

GAP BETWEEN GOAL AND PERFORMANCE _50% to be trained. All located outside headquarters in satellite offices._

CAUSES	FINDINGS
Do employees have the skills and knowledge to meet the performance goals?	_No; only 50% at headquarters_
Do employees know the performance standards or expectations?	_Yes; announced in bulletin_
Do employees receive feedback about their performance?	_Yes_
Do employees have the necessary resources to perform?	_Yes; will provide required training_
Do employees receive appropriate incentives to perform?	_Yes, profit sharing per group performance_

Source: Adapted from Steadman, S.V. (1980). Learning to Select a Needs Assessment Strategy. _Training and Development Journal._ Alexandria: American Society for Training & Development.

There are other good reasons to conduct a needs analysis before actually developing a training program. When you design training activities, it is extremely helpful to obtain case material directly from the workplace or participants' personal situations. Armed with this information, you can base your designs on real issues that participants face, rather than on simulated material.

How to Collect Information. As you think about the kind of information that would be useful, consider first asking the potential participants to identify their needs. By going directly to the participants for the information prior to the training intervention, you give them a role in designing and developing their own program. Your involvement at this early stage also enables you to develop a relationship with the participants and their supervisors and managers. Because they appreciate your involvement, they are likely to be receptive to the program, which increases the likelihood of its success.

If you cannot collect information directly from each person in your target audience, consider the following two options:

- Send a questionnaire to participants before meeting them. This provides you with an opportunity to tell them about yourself and your plans for the upcoming program, and it helps you to learn about them.

- Phone or visit some or all the participants for an assessment interview. This option provides the opportunity for face-to-face interaction and minimizes awkward feelings when you meet in the classroom at the start of the program.

Advantages and disadvantages of collecting information by observation and questionnaires are outlined in table 5.

There are three primary sources of training needs: people, the job, and the organization, as table 6 shows. A source internal to the organization means that someone or something within your organization brings the problem or issue to your attention. A source external to the organization means that a person, place, or thing not within your organization brings the problem or issue to your attention.

Often the first sign that training might be needed surfaces as a specific problem within one of the three primary sources. You then need to define the problem in more depth. You must decide if the problem is

Table 5. Advantages and disadvantages of observation and questionnaires.

OBSERVATION	ADVANTAGES	DISADVANTAGES
Can be as technical as time-motion studies or as functionally or behaviorally specific as observing a new board or staff members interacting during a meeting.	Minimizes interruption of routine work flow or group activity.	Requires a highly skilled observer with both process and content knowledge (unlike an interviewer who needs, for the most part, only process skills).
May be as unstructured as walking through an agency's offices on the lookout for evidence of communication barriers.	Generates in situ data, highly relevant to the situation where response to identified training needs and interests will have an impact.	Carries limitations because able to collect data only within the work setting (flip side of the first advantage).
Can be used normatively to distinguish between effective and ineffective behaviors, organizational structures, and/or process.	Provides important comparison checks between the observer's and the respondent's inferences (when combined with a feedback step).	
QUESTIONNAIRES	**ADVANTAGES**	**DISADVANTAGES**
May be surveys or polls of a random or stratified sample of respondents, or an enumeration of an entire population.	Reaches a large number of people in a short time.	Makes little provision for free expression of unanticipated responses.
Can use a variety of question formats: open ended, projective, forced choice, priority-ranking.	Is relatively inexpensive.	Requires substantial time (and technical skills, especially in survey model) for developing effective instruments.
Can take alternative forms such as rating scales, either predesigned or self-generated by one or more respondents.	Provides opportunity for expressing self without fear of embarrassment.	Are of limited utility in getting at causes or problems or possible solutions.
May be self-administered (by mail) under controlled or uncontrolled conditions, or may require the presence of an interpreter or assistant.	Yields data that can be easily summarized and reported.	Suffers low return rates (mailed), grudging responses, or unintended and/or inappropriate respondents.

Source: Adapted from Steadman, S.V. (1980). Learning to Select a Needs Assessment Strategy. *Training and Development Journal.* Alexandria: American Society for Training & Development.

Table 6. Sources of training needs.

SOURCE	INTERNAL TO ORGANIZATION	EXTERNAL TO ORGANIZATION
People	Potential trainers Supervisors Upper-level managers	Trainers in other organizations Outside consultants
Job	Personnel changes (new hires, promotions) Job task changes Changes in performance standards Equipment changes Analyses of efficiency indexes (e.g., waste, downtime, repairs, quality control)	Professional associations Outside consultants Government regulations
Organization	Changes in the organization's mission Mergers and acquisitions Change in organizational structure New products and services Analysis of organizational climate (e.g., grievances, absenteeism, turnover, accidents)	Government regulations and legislative mandate Outside consultants Pressure from outside competition Environmental pressures (e.g., political, economic, demographic, technical)

Source: Reprinted with permission from Caffarella, Rosemary. (1988). *Program Development and Evaluation Resource Book for Trainers.*

- performance related
- short or long term
- new or recurring
- affecting a few or many employees
- urgent, important, or unimportant.

By defining the problem, you are able to target it and prioritize your response. Generally, if the problem affects a few people, deal with the few. Find out what's going on and determine what should be going on. Determine if the issue is urgent and to whom it is urgent. Find out how the stakeholders want it resolved and when. If it doesn't seem urgent, determine who the stakeholders are and how they want the issue resolved.

If the problem is short term, for example, you might rectify it by developing a mechanism that uses a job aid, or you might meet with a group of people involved with it. If the problem is new or recurring, you might have to devote training resources to investigate it.

Is training appropriate? Use the data summary sheet in figure 6 to guide your decision about the appropriateness of training intervention.

When there is no time to conduct an analysis, do the following:

- Phone a contact person who is familiar with the participants. Use the audience analysis and the problem analysis profile sheets.

- Introduce yourself and ask participants via telephone some key questions. Trust the responses to be representative and treat them as if they were a sample of the large group. Or ask a contact person to schedule a phone interview for you.

- Ensure that you receive relevant materials (such as surveys, meeting notes, records).

- Obtain opinions and impressions from other trainers who have worked with the training group.

Figure 6. Data summary sheet.

1. Outline the problem or need in the organization for which you believe a training intervention might be appropriate. Be as specific as possible.

2. Determine whether the need or problem you have identified is performance related and why or why not. If the need or problem is related to performance, go to number 3. If the need or problem is not related to performance, go to number 5.

3. Is this a macro or micro problem? What action are you suggesting?

4. Classify the need or problem you have identified as something your employees (check one):
   a. do not know (lack of knowledge) ..... ☐
   b. cannot do (lack of skill) .... ☐
   c. can do, but aren't movtivated to do ... ☐

   If it is a lack of skill or knowledge, then a training activity is an appropriate intervention. If you have classified it as a lack of motivation, go to number 5.

5. Identify possible solutions to the problem or need other than training. List these alternatives.

- Talk to participants who arrive early and obtain whatever information you can.

- Design some activities at the beginning of the program to enable you to assess the group.

- If you conducted some front-end analysis and designed your program on the basis of your analysis results, you should be able to make final adjustments before the training meeting begins.

Step Three: Analysis

In this phase you will take all the information you collected through your investigation, step two, and organize it in various ways to analyze the information. Several analytical techniques exist. Before beginning to undertake the rigors of analysis, you should review figure 6, the data summary sheet, and record the information according to the source, required skill set or sets, and the type of need (educational or training), and you should establish priorities. Use the data summary sheet organizer in table 7 to sort the information collected from the data summary sheets.

In recording information about the job, break down a job or function into tasks to pinpoint where the training or performance need exists. Several methods are available to help you identify the job tasks. You can review job literature, observe job performance, and question people on the job. The form in table 8 provides one way to record responses to questions from an on-site observation or interview that can provide information

Table 7. Data summary sheet organizer.				
SOURCE	**EVIDENCE OF NEED**	**SKILLS SET(S)**	**EDUCATION or TRAINING**	**PRIORITY**
Organization	*Satellite offices*	*Coding*	*Upgrade coding procedure*	*High*
People	*Finance staff in billing office of satellite*	*Analyzing and critical thinking*		
Job	*Accounts or billing*			

about the tasks that are performed. In that example, interviews at a satellite office showed a need to upgrade training in coding for accounts (billing).

Use the information in table 3 to direct you to the tasks being performed. You can then review the two tables in concert to be sure you've examined each task. In some cases, you may determine that it isn't necessary to do an on-site observation because it may be obvious that the problem can be rectified without training.

At this point, you will have broken down the functional responsibilities into tasks. You now validate the job analysis with an advisory group made up of subject matter experts, management representatives, and client contacts to guarantee that the job analysis matches the job. Ask the advisory group to help select the key functions and tasks that will be the focus of your training course. It is often necessary to select key tasks because there is not enough time to prepare training for everything that was uncovered in a job analysis.

Present Findings. There are several ways to present findings: check sheets, line graphs, and Pareto charts. Check sheets are easy to design and use. As table 9 shows, check sheets use hash marks to show the frequency of a number of events. A check sheet allows you to decide what events to record, determine the time period for the observation (for example, hours, days, months), and develop the format. Information from check sheets is easily transferable to a frequency graph.

TASK	**HOW FREQUENTLY DO YOU PERFORM THIS TASK?**			**WHERE DID YOU FIRST LEARN HOW TO PERFORM THIS TASK?**				**HOW CRITICAL IS THIS TASK TO YOUR JOB?**			**WHAT IS THE BEST WAY TO LEARN THIS TASK?**		
	Never	Sometimes	Often	On the job	School	Training	Other	Very	Somewhat	Not very	On the job	Training	Other
1 Coding			✔	✔				✔			✔		
2													
3													
4													
5													
6													

Table 8. Sample job analysis questionnaire.

DELAY	SEPTEMBER				TOTAL
	3	4	5	6	
Missing information	//	/	///	//	8
Policy changes/questions	////	//// //	////	//// ///	24
Input errors	//// ////	//// //// ///	//// //	//// ////	38
Alerts/routing		/	//	/	4
Individual work habits	//	///	//	///	10
Total	18	25	18	23	84

Table 9. Sample check sheet.

Source: McArdle, G.E.H. (1998). *Conducting a Needs Assessment.* Menlo Park, CA: Crisp Publications, p. 64.

A line graph displays trends in a particular activity over a specific time period, as figure 7 shows. Use the line graph to track a specific activity or activities over a period of time to identify changes as soon as they occur. By noting the change immediately, you can recommend taking prompt action.

A Pareto chart is a bar chart. The bar chart displays the relative importance of different events or needs. The most frequent events or greatest needs (the higher the numbers) appear to the left of the chart. The Pareto chart is similar to the check sheet in its ability to identify root causes of problems.

Take Action. Once the organization has developed a clear picture of the training priorities, the next step is to decide the best way to meet the needs. The organization has several options:

- Design, develop, and deliver the training program in-house.
- Contract with an outside consultant to design and develop the coursework for in-house delivery.
- Contract with an outside training facility to handle all aspects of the training.
- Purchase a commercially marketed training program and train in-house staff to teach the program

Organizations without in-house training departments usually have to look outside for all but the most basic type of on-the-job training pro-

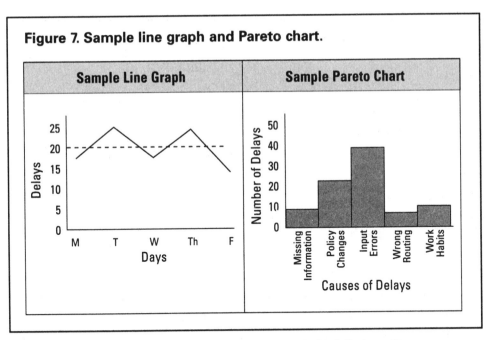

Figure 7. Sample line graph and Pareto chart.

Source: McArdle, G.E.H. (1998). *Conducting a Needs Assessment.* Menlo Park, CA: Crisp Publications, p. 65.

grams. For organizations that have internal training staff, the decision is more complex. Answers to the following questions can help narrow the choice:

- How often and to how many employees will the training program be offered?
- Do we have a content expert with credible delivery skills?
- Will the training program address a one-time need targeted to only a few employees, or will the program take place only a few times a year?
- Will training involve generic skills or a specific technical need?
- Will the trainees be lower-level staff or upper-level managers?
- Will the content of the program involve proprietary or competitive information?

In thinking about the questions, consider the cost-effectiveness of a training intervention. If training will be infrequent, it may be more cost-effective to use an outside consultant. Alternatively, ongoing training needed by many employees may be more cost-effective if developed and delivered in-house. When training involves technology, equipment, or skills unique to the organization and its jobs, in-house design and delivery may be the only option. For top management, a consultant's polished presentation and broad range of experience with other companies enhance the program's credibility. For lower-level positions, trainees may view a program as more relevant and credible if it is developed and delivered by someone familiar with day-to-day problems. If the content of the training program is proprietary, again, developing and delivering the program in-house is probably preferred.

Negotiate Training Objectives. Training program objectives should be clearly stated to ensure they include those critical activities or performance issues that will be accepted as evidence that the participants learned something. Training should follow the sequence of the objectives so that learning occurs in a logical progression.

There are two types of objectives—terminal and enabling.

- Terminal objectives describe what a training program participant will be able to do at the end of the training program and under what conditions and at what level of competence the participant must perform. Terminal objectives are the cornerstone of a training program because training program developers, instructors, participants, clients, and evaluators all use them.
- Enabling objectives flow from the major task statements (for example, output, nature of the organization). These types of objectives represent the basic skills, knowledge, and attitudes that must be learned before meeting the course objective.

Design Training and Course Module. The instructional specifications serve as a blueprint for program development. They are guidelines for content, timing of presentation of ideas, and reasons the content is included. The completed program can then be compared to the blueprint when the training course is evaluated.

Specifying instructional content is a joint effort by training and subject matter experts. In this part of the analysis, the critical content of the modules is defined systematically. The instructional strategy used when introducing the content, determining appropriate learning techniques, providing opportunities for practice, and determining the appropriate media forms must be clearly defined as well. All media selected should have a definite purpose.

Instructional specifications include the following:

- module name
- introduction
  — content summary
  — utility
  — importance

- sequence of topics and activities
  — flow
  — transitions
  — links

- objectives
  — special teaching point
  — media requirements
  — testing requirement
  — learner/trainer activities.

Need for Ongoing Needs Analysis. An effective training department must continually plan, design, deliver, and assess its training intervention. The following steps provide a useful strategy.

- Step one: Assess ongoing training. What training do employees need? What new skills will the organization need in the future? Conduct an annual needs survey. Rank the identified needs and concentrate on those first by developing a six-month or yearlong training agenda. Some typical categories of training topics follow.
  — health and safety topics
  — sales and customer service training
  — clerical, technical, and specialized, interpersonal, or managerial skills
  — professional development programs such as career and personal development
  — succession planning.

- Step two: Design training programs. Determine the following for each training program you develop:
  — course objectives
  — test items

- instructional methods
- material content
- course and module design
- training program length
- method for identifying participants
- trainer and program management
- budget
- training announcement
- registration and confirmation process.

- Step three: Design training course and sample module and course module. Before beginning the training program, sell the program to employees and management. Meet with selected instructors to ensure the training goal is consistent with your design and instructional methodology. Check the materials, logistics, and evaluation mechanism.

- Step four: Create the training report. Before beginning to design a training intervention, you must describe clearly your training concept and secure management's approval.

- Step five: Return to step one.

Choose Trainers. Organizations that choose to deliver training in-house must decide who should conduct the training sessions. Large organizations may have a fully qualified staff of training professionals who can handle most teaching assignments. Smaller organizations, however, will need to locate a qualified staff person or outside trainer to handle the assignment.

In-House Personnel. For many types of training, qualified course instructors can be found within the organization. Each executive, for instance, has expertise in a certain area, and most can make time to conduct at least one or two training sessions. Other potential instructors include supervisors and managers; human resource personnel, especially those with career counseling and similar experience; and professional employees, particularly ones who have had previous teaching experience.

Outside Trainers. Part- and full-time faculty at area colleges and universities are ideal candidates to recruit as trainers. Depending on the nature of the course, other outside professionals to consider as either instructors or guest speakers include consultants, lawyers, psychologists, systems analysts, or efficiency experts. Professional and trade associations as well as local chambers of commerce may be able to provide you with the names of experts who would be willing to make presentations.

Step Four: Reporting

This final step in conducting a needs analysis is your opportunity to present your work from the first three steps. By organizing the information from surveillance and investigation and discussing your interpretations from analysis, you can now succinctly and clearly convince management that the training intervention you propose will solve the identified problem or problems and respond to management's request. Communicating the results in writing and in a spoken presentation usually improves chances for success.

The training design report defines and documents findings of the needs analysis process and summarizes the problem statement, the analyses used to determine the training need, and a proposed module design. In the final report, discuss how your findings relate to the organization's overall strategy and goals and how the proposed change or training program will benefit the organization and the employees.

Training Design Report. Aimed at a wide audience, many of whom may not be familiar with the topic, and written in simple, clear language, a training design report summarizes the results of the investigation and analysis, communicates progress to key management, and provides the training manager with material for supervising each stage of the project. The following eight components make up a training design report:

- *Purpose of proposed course:* Describes the training problem, the training format, and the history of the problem within the organization. Keep this section to one paragraph.

- *Summary of analysis:* Summarizes the need; defines clearly the performance gaps that the proposed training will address; describes the audience; and explains the job, the tasks that make up that job, and the key performance elements needed to fulfill the job requirements. An extensive description is needed because the performance gap is probably located either in a task, a performance element of the task, or a lack or misunderstanding of the knowledge the participants need to perform the task.

- *Scope of the course:* Establishes the format for the course. Presents an overview of the materials that will be used, the content or topics and subtopics, and the instructional strategies that will be used in delivering the course.

- *Learning objectives:* Presents the learning objective statements that will guide the course and the learning.

- *Test item strategy:* Describes how the participants will demonstrate mastery of the topic. Discusses how you will conduct the testing and why and what happens after the testing. For example, if the participants fail a test item, you should decide if the test item should be rewritten or determine if the training materials are problematic.

- *Course and module design:* Provides the instructional methods; the length of the course; and the training format, timing, and location.

- *Delivery strategy:* Outlines the instructional methods; the length of the course; and the training format, timing, and location.

- *Evaluation or measurement tools:* Explains your evaluation mechanism and how you are going to measure the participants' reactions to the training, their learning (meaning the results of the test items), and their behavior (meaning how the concepts will be mastered).

Final Report. Again, using clear, concise language, a final report presents the results of all phases of the needs analysis. The report will identify performance gaps between the position in question and the function of the position. The final report includes the complete picture of what needs to be changed, how changes will be made, and how the organization and individuals will be affected by the changes. Think of the final report as the final sales presentation to all levels of the organization. The following nine components make up the final report:

- *Executive summary:* This first section is critical. The executive summary should be short—one page is best—and should answer the question, "If readers are too busy to look at the entire report, what's the least amount of information they need to make an informed decision?"

- *Objectives of the needs analysis:* Provides the opportunity to explain in detail the objectives of the needs analysis. What information did you hope to learn in conducting a needs analysis of the organization or of a particular department?

- *Brief summary of findings:* Discusses optimal performance (what the organization hopes to achieve), actual performance (the organization's current level of performance), and how to bridge the gap between the two.

- *Proposed change or training project:* Explains clearly the commitment involved. How much will the program cost? How long will it take to complete? How long will it be before we see results? Who will be involved? How will the program be implemented? What resources are needed for the program to succeed?

- *Data-collection methods:* Explains why you collected the data you did and the process you used to analyze data and information.

- *Expanded discussion of findings:* Discusses study results in detail. However, unless you have prepared the presentation for highly analytical thinkers, you may want to present findings in a descriptive form. You can include simple tables and graphs, but also describe the results in words. Save copies of the actual questionnaires for an appendix to the report.

- *Implications and analysis:* Discusses the implications of your results. Relates the data to the organization's objectives.

- *Recommendations for future action:* Presents specific recommendations for future action. Recommendations should include at least the skills, knowledge, and attitudes required for a particular position, a training strategy (what a training program might look like; in other words, a module design in graphic form), and other issues you uncovered that management should resolve before proceeding with the proposed change or training program or concurrently with the program.

- *Appendices of supporting data:* Includes relevant supporting data such as sample surveys and other data collection methods, detailed analysis of the results, a cost breakdown, and a timeline of the proposed change.

It is critical that you know your audience when you are presenting your findings orally. As much as possible, learn about their values, attitudes, and needs. The presentation should focus on answering the question, What's in it for me?

Follow these tips when you work with 35-mm slides, computer shows, or overhead transparencies (all called *frame* in this section):

- Use a few words per frame.
- Use pleasing and easy-to-see colors, such as blue as foreground or background, rather than yellow, which fades, or red, which is difficult to read.
- Use some type of bulleted list.
- Use graphics or images.
- Keep charts and graphs simple.

You, not the frames, are the show. The oral presentation reinforces the material provided in the written reports.

SUMMARY AND HIGHLIGHTS

Analysis is a key element in the training process. It is the first step and is a critical step. For a successful training program, ensure that you:

- Define your role as the trainer.
- Remember the six strategies for success—management commitment, rationale for training intervention, questions that guide the process, factors that influence the process, types of intervention, and performance standards and criteria.
- Identify learners' needs.
- Follow the four-step needs analysis process—surveillance (scan the organization to determine if there is a need or performance gap); investigation (determine the type of data you need to guide your decision about a training intervention and determine the data collection method); analysis (obtain a clear picture of the problem, the evidence, and the data sources to help determine the type of problem and determine the best source for training—using in-house personnel, hiring consultants, or

purchasing a complete package); and report (written and oral presentation to management about your findings).

- Consider time, need, timeliness, and cause and effect when conducting your needs analysis. Remember, your goal is to develop a well-defined problem statement during the surveillance stage; then identify the problem by gathering information in the investigation step; then analyze the information collected; and finally, report your findings.

4

Design

INTRODUCTION

Given the analysis that we have just gone through, you have enough information to prepare a preliminary budget. This budget will help you decide if you are going to purchase a generic program from a vendor or if you are going to custom design the program. The basis for the budget is the amount of hours of design time, the size of the audience, and the frequency of the presentation. If the program would be for a small number of people, you could send them for training or could have an expert provide training at your organization for a few hours or a day.

If at this stage it appears that you will be designing the program, you must take many factors into account. Some factors will apply at the outset. As the designer, you will determine others, and as you train, you will determine still others. In most cases, the information you collected during the analysis stage will help you in this process. If not, use your creativity to fill in the gaps.

After completing the needs analysis, you will know if the issue initially brought to your attention is a training problem or not, and if the problem is a training problem, what the trainees need to learn. This chapter presents the building blocks for your training. Learning objectives are defined as models of learning theory. Once you have clarified the objectives and decided on which model of learning theory is relevant, you can select the content and organize learning modules.

PREPARE LEARNING OBJECTIVES

Learning objectives may be the most critical input in designing training sessions. People are more likely to complete training sessions successfully if they are told at the outset of the session what the goals of the training are.

When designing training sessions, take a cue from textbook planners. The beginning of most textbook chapters lists the learning goals for that chapter. More than likely, the chapter was designed around these learning goals or learning objectives. This means that the author organized the material or content, including examples and exercises, in sequences that best match the learning objectives, just as trainers use the set of objectives for the session to determine and direct the design of the session.

Objectives are tools that point to the content and procedures that will lead to successful instruction, help you manage the actual instructional process, and help you prepare methods for finding out whether the instruction succeeded. Some objectives are useful, whereas others serve no purpose. A useful objective succeeds in communicating an instructional intent to the trainees and paints a picture of a successful learner. It pinpoints your intent and excludes other possible meanings.

Our language is full of fuzzy words that can be interpreted in a number of ways. Although it may be useful to use fuzzy words in some situations, it isn't useful in training. If you state the objectives using fuzzy words, you leave the training open to a wide range of interpretations. Just as most of you would not want to be skewered with a "What do you mean by that?" every time you said "Have a good day," most of you would not want to leave your specific instructional objectives open to misunderstanding.

When designing the training program, state three types of objectives:

- what the training will accomplish for the organization
- what the training will accomplish for the trainees
- how accomplishments will be measured.

When stating objectives, use terms that are not open to misunderstanding to ensure that people in a training program know what is expected of them at completion of the program. For example, an objective that states, "At the end of this workshop, you will be able to install an XYZ window air conditioning unit without assistance," is more informative than one that says, "At the end of this workshop, you will know how to install an XYZ window air conditioning unit." Table 1 compares several fuzzy words with specific words.

Table 1. Fuzzy wording versus specific language.	
FUZZY WORDS	**SPECIFIC WORDS**
Know	Write
Understand	Recite
Understand fully	Identify
Appreciate	Sort
Appreciate fully	Solve
Grasp the significance of	Construct
Enjoy	Build
Believe	Compare
Internalize	Contrast

For objectives to communicate and be useful, they must have certain characteristics. Trainers use several different schemes to state well-defined objectives. Regardless of your experience as a trainer, you would be well advised to use the format that follows to create objectives. The format works and is easy to use.

The format includes three characteristics—performance, condition, criterion—each of which when posed as a question communicates an objective or behavioral intent.

- *Performance.* What should the learner be able to do? An objective always says what a learner is expected to do as a result of the training. The performance is always the verb.

- *Condition.* Under what conditions do you want the learner to be able to perform? An objective always describes the important conditions, if any, under which performance is to occur. The condition is always the resources.

- *Criterion.* How well must the learner perform? Whenever possible, an objective describes how well the learner must perform to be considered acceptable. Thus, all objectives must be designed to be specific, measurable, and observable.

Table 2 shows how this format works for the following examples.

- Using the given equipment, the trainee must be able to execute three quarter-inch sutures within one minute.
- Given the formal training report format, write a three-to-five-page training needs analysis report covering all the report components that meets the trainers' specifications.

Can you provide three examples of objectives for different learning situations using this format?

Most training sessions are intended to accomplish a variety of goals. Usually trainers have some new information, a procedure, a policy, or a theory to impart to trainees. Trainers often want trainees to develop skills in using that information on the job to solve problems, make decisions, carry out tasks, and so on. Sometimes trainers are interested in changing attitudes and values or in increasing sensitivity or tolerance.

Articulating the training goals would not be so critical if trainers could pursue all of them in essentially the same way. However, research on learning indicates that different types of goals require different teaching methods and learning activities, as is described later.

Identify Objectives

The success or effectiveness of the training you design relates directly to the instructional objectives. If a reason for the learning exists, then you must clearly specify the training or instructional objectives.

	PERFORMANCE	CONDITION	CRITERION
Table 2. Characteristics of the objectives planning tool.			
Example 1	executive three-quarter-inch sutures	the given equipment	within one minute
Example 2	write a three-to-five-page training needs analysis report	given the formal training report format	meets the trainer's specifications

There are two strategies for communicating objectives: provide statements of behavioral objectives and provide topical objectives.

Provide behavioral objectives that do the following:

- delineate to some extent what trainees are expected to know when they begin the training
- specify the nature and quantity of new information to be provided by the training program
- specify the desired results (that is, the behavior that is to occur once training has been completed successfully)
- indicate the time and conditions needed to carry out the training program and implement the behavioral changes
- indicate how the behavioral change will be measured, including the circumstances under which the outcome will be measured along with a statement of minimum acceptable performance (for example, how well or how fast a task is to be performed)
- include caveats, restrictions, and limitations related to any or all of the above, if appropriate.

Following is an example of a well-defined objective: Using the map reference guide, name correctly every item shown on each of the 20 blueprints in 20 minutes.

One example of a poorly stated objective is as follows: Understand the functions of all calculators after one lesson.

Topical objectives should tell participants what they are about to learn. An objective might say, for example, that participants will be able to use the new inventory system and have an overall knowledge of how the system functions.

Practice Objectives

People are more likely to accomplish the objectives if they are given opportunities to practice the behaviors identified in them. If trainees are to use the new information to make decisions, they need opportunities during the training course to practice decision making.

There are three types of practice:

- concentrated, in which practice takes place during a concentrated time period to increase the efficiency of learning new information, concepts, principles, or skills

- distributed, in which practice takes place over a period of time to increase retention
- varied, in which practice takes place in a variety of settings.

Writing Specific Objectives

By writing specific behavioral objectives, you make it easier to measure what the trainees learn. To learn if the objective is specific, ask the following five questions about it:

1. Who is to perform the task?
2. What category of learning is involved?
3. What is the terminal behavior (for example, skill)?
4. Under what conditions will it be demonstrated?
5. What degree or level of proficiency is to be met to succeed?

Extensive educational research has accepted a model of three major learning categories:

- *Skills (psychomotor):* Psychomotor ability is the muscular actions that employees use in performing their jobs, such as writing and operating equipment. Skills can be observed and, therefore, are easily quantifiable.
- *Knowledge (cognitive):* Cognitive ability is what employees know in order to perform, such as the principles of accounting. Knowledge is not easily quantifiable.
- *Attitudes (affective):* Affective ability is what employees bring to the job in terms of feelings. How people feel about what they do and about the organization for which they are working affects their performance.

An objective written in the psychomotor domain will specify that trainees will develop a skill or skills. It will require that trainees coordinate their brains with physical activity.

An objective written in the cognitive domain will state that the training is designed to enable trainees to know or understand something. After the session, trainees will be able to point the something out, describe the something, recognize the something, or define the something.

An objective in the affective domain will use verbs that connote feelings and emotions, such as *respect, cooperate,* and *enjoy.*

Some time after delivering the training, you can evaluate the trainees' performance relative to your original objectives. Now you must decide how you want to create the means for getting there—the design. Later you can arrange to find out whether you arrived, as chapter seven, "Evaluation," will explain.

If the training fails, the objectives may have been unclear or unrelated to on-the-job performance. Training may also fail because elements based on adult learning principles were missing or were poorly integrated into the design. Effective training requires some understanding of adult learning principles.

UNDERSTAND ADULT LEARNING

Adults vary greatly in the following areas:

- knowledge about their work
- pride in their work
- motivation to perform better
- maturity
- security
- learning styles
- expectations about the trainer
- expectations about what the training will do for them.

The last may be the most important of these areas. For training to be effective, trainees must believe that it is for them and not simply to increase their employer's productivity or to fulfill their manager's obligation to provide training programs.

Adult learners may enter their first training session with expectations similar to those they had when they were in school. Much more is expected of adult learners in that well-designed training involves trainees actively in the learning process. Adult learning styles vary. Training experts have found the following general approaches useful when designing training for the learner:

- Focus on real world problems.

- Emphasize how trainees can apply what they are learning.

- Relate the learning to the trainees' goals.

- Relate the materials and new knowledge presented to the trainees' experience.

- Allow trainees to debate and to challenge ideas.

- Listen to and respect trainees' opinions.

Adult Learning Theory

There are no right or wrong ways to absorb new information. The methods by which people learn are complex. More than likely your trainees will be one of the following types of learner: confident, affective, transitional, integrated, or risk taking.

Confident Learners

Characteristically, confident learners want to know why they are assigned particular tasks. Tasks assigned to confident learners must have a clear purpose. If they are given the opportunity, confident learners will set their own goals and may even help set direction for the training session. Confident learners like to be involved and consulted and will happily respond to a request to identify a certain number of issues, problems, or themes on which they would like the training to focus. In some cases, trainers can use confident learners to help decide what content would be relevant and meaningful.

Confident learners sometimes prepare in advance for training sessions and may very well be irritated by trainers who progress too slowly, have less than well-defined objectives, or do not seek input from the trainees. Confident learners may be potential leaders and need opportunities for interactive learning. Group discussions, team projects, and shared experiences appeal to confident learners as do learning from peers and helping peers learn. Confident learners prefer training sessions that lead to specific goals. These learners may actually confront trainers whose programs or techniques appear inadequate, but they will not threaten well-prepared trainers.

Affective Learners

Affective learners like to know and feel that they are doing fine. Affective learners are influenced by their feelings. They want to feel an attachment to their trainers, and they expect the trainers to be experts who are paid to explain, synthesize, and decrease the complexity of a subject. Affective learners want to be invited to participate and can be counted on for their patience, endurance, and loyalty when the path to reaching a learning goal might seem long and circuitous to others.

To best reach affective learners, trainers should do the following:

- provide clearly written assignments or clearly defined exercises
- encourage enjoyable learning activities such as interaction with other adults who value training
- specify particular reference books for further information
- recognize that these learners will strive to fulfill the trainers' reasonable and well-defined expectations.

Transitional Learners

Transitional learners are those who are being promoted or moving horizontally to a new job. These learners tend to focus more than others on the particular type of information they are learning and on how that learning will apply to their new situations. Transitional learners, in general, may be apprehensive about making job changes and may want to tell trainers either about the work experience or environment from which they are coming or the work experience or environment to which they are moving. Transitional learners need to be reassured that they are fully capable of learning and succeeding. Trainers can do so by inviting these learners to discuss training objectives and techniques.

Transitional learners tend to see everything as potentially new and highly relevant. Many of them may not yet be familiar with all aspects of their new work environment. To best appeal to these learners, challenge them to learn. Transitional learners may not expect everything that is covered in the training session to have simple, obvious, and conclusive outcomes.

Integrated Learners

Integrated learners present a particularly interesting challenge to trainers because more often than not they establish peerlike relationships with trainers. Integrated learners are not satisfied merely to receive information, they want to do something with the information they receive. Integrated learners know where they want to go, enjoy being responsible for their own learning, and want freedom (within some structure) to accomplish specific tasks and assignments without much outside guidance.

Integrated learners are self-directed and demand quality from others as well as themselves. They want their work to be good and well integrated with overall objectives. Because integrated learners know what they want to learn and have used processes to learn on their own, trainers do not need to tell them precisely how to undertake specific learning tasks.

Risk-Taking Learners

Risk-taking learners thrive on learning new skills and information. They like to deviate from traditional course content and techniques, and to change their routines and schedules. In general, risk-taking learners are willing to work hard to meet goals, particularly if they will benefit from learning new concepts. Risk-taking learners will stray from course guidelines happily if straying presents an opportunity to gain new knowledge.

Trainers can use the emerging design (see description in the "Types of Training Design" section) for risk-taking learners. Trainers need not be concerned if they have sketchy materials because risk-taking learners will welcome the opportunity for interactive exercises.

ADULT LEARNING PRINCIPLES

Adult learning principles provide a framework for development that helps ensure that participants learn. The acronym *LEARN* is useful in remembering some of these aspects of adult learning.

- *L*earner directed: If adults understand why they need the information you give them, the lesson will be easier for them to learn.

- *E*xperiential: Adults in a learning environment gain more from experiencing the concepts being taught than they do from just a lecture or presentation. They want active involvement and relevance to their job and organization. This involves practicing and applying the concepts rather than lecture only.

- *A*ble to be evaluated: When teaching a concept, define it. Specify as clearly as possible the result you want from the learners. Identify what change in knowledge, skill, or attitude will take place.

- *R*esidual: Adults learn more effectively if they build on known information, facts, or experiences rather than from independent, arbitrary facts. Base the information provided on their experience and knowledge and lead them into more depth of knowledge.

- *Numerous instructional methods:* Some people learn better from verbal instructions, some from written instructions, and some from example; others are visually oriented, and still others learn by trial and error. To reach a wider audience, incorporate various methods in the program because they provide valuable reinforcement and make learning more interesting.

Learning Principles

You must be familiar with the following 10 learning principles to design and develop appropriate interventions: part or whole learning, spaced learning, active learning, feedback, overlearning, reinforcement, primacy and recency, meaningful material, multiple-sense learning, and transfer of learning. A description of each of these principles appears in the sections that follow.

Part Learning or Whole Learning

Part learning is more common than whole learning because trainees prefer dealing with a series of separate assignments. In part learning, the skill or knowledge would be divided into parts or segments. In whole learning, they would be looked at as a large, unified block of material. When dividing the material into segments, the trainer should use two guidelines:

- The segments should not be too large. Although it's familiar to you, the material will be new to the trainees. Therefore, review the skill or knowledge from the trainees' perspective, and then organize it into segments for training.
- Segments should follow a logical sequence. Put the material in an appropriate sequence so the trainees can relate each part to the next. A logical flow will enhance learners' ability to recall the skill or information. Proceed from the known to the unknown, moving from one segment to the next after you know by the trainees' behavior that they have understood and accepted the information. (Caution: Do not oversimplify. After separating the material into segments and developing a logical

sequence, check to make sure the segments are not so small as to be boring.)

As an example of whole learning, consider teaching someone to ride a bicycle. This training should be divided into three parts: balancing, steering, and pedaling. Learning each part independently would be difficult because steering depends on balancing and on how hard the pedals are pushed, and balancing depends on steering and pedaling. Teaching someone to ride a bicycle requires whole learning. Whole learning is fairly uncommon; most training models are based on part learning.

Spaced Learning

Spaced learning usually is superior to crammed learning if trainees are to retain the material long-term. Spaced learning has its basis in what we know about incubation. The brain needs time to assimilate a particular group of facts before it can accept the next group of facts. Spaced learning creates opportunities for regular review and revision, which slow down the rate at which trainees forget material.

Active Learning

Involving trainees actively in the training rather than having them listen passively encourages trainees to become self-motivated. Active learning is more effective than passive learning and is often described as learning by doing. Provide trainees plenty of opportunity to practice using the skills and information they are learning.

Feedback

The feedback principle of learning has two aspects:

- Trainees need constructive feedback on their progress.
- Trainers need feedback on their own performance.

Feedback to trainees can vary in complexity from explaining why an answer is correct or incorrect to commenting on trainees' performance doing an activity or discussing results of a test. Regardless of the complexity of the feedback, the best feedback is the one given the earliest. The more immediate the feedback, the greater its value, especially for preventing loss of self-confidence and, thus, loss of motivation.

Feedback to trainers answers the following questions:

- Are trainees receiving and understanding the information? (Test trainees for this.)
- Do trainees have doubts or questions? (Ask them.)
- Are all the trainees paying attention? (Observe them.)
- Is the session boring? (Observe them.)
- Would trainees benefit by using more techniques during this session? (Ask them.)

Two-way communication is critical to feedback's effectiveness.

Overlearning

Overlearning means learning until trainees have near perfect recall, and then learning the material just a bit more, perhaps through practice. Overlearning decreases the rate of forgetting. In other words, forgetting is significantly reduced by frequent recall or use of the material. Two important facts will help you:

- Trainers' repetition does not maximize retention.
- Trainees' active involvement maximizes retention.

Reinforcement

Reinforcement is one way to improve learning because learning that is rewarded is much more likely to be retained. A simple, "Yes, that's right," can mean a great deal to trainees and can enhance their retention considerably. Positive reinforcement confirms the value of responding and participating and encourages active learning, whereas negative reinforcement simply tells trainees that their responses were wrong without providing guidelines about which responses would have been correct. Negative reinforcement often discourages trainees from further investigation.

Primacy and Recency

When they are presented with a sequence of information, trainees tend to remember what they heard first and what they heard last, but they often forget what they heard in the middle. To guard against this, emphasize and reinforce facts that are in the middle or present critical information at the beginning or end of the session.

Meaningful Material

Unconsciously, trainees ask two questions when presented with new information:

- Is this information valid relative to my experiences?
- Will this information be useful in the immediate future?

The first question emphasizes the notion of moving from the known to the unknown as well as the fact that people tend to remember material that relates to what they already know. In designing the training session, make sure to assess trainees' current level of learning.

The second question emphasizes the fact that trainees want to know that what they are about to learn will be useful to them in the near future. Meaningful material links the past and the future and promotes two beneficial effects: security (when trainees move from the known to the unknown) and motivation (information will be useful in the near future).

Multiple-Sense Learning

Research suggests that of the information people absorb, they will obtain approximately 80 percent through sight, 11 percent through hearing, and 9 percent through all other senses combined. Therefore, to absorb as much as possible, trainers should design sessions to use two or more of the senses. Sight and hearing are straightforward, but designing sessions to use other senses, such as touch, might be just as crucial to successful learning. For most learning, however, sight provides the most information, so trainers should emphasize visual aids when designing their sessions. (For more on visual aids, see chapter six, "Implementation.")

Transfer of Learning

The amount of learning that trainees transfer from the training room to the workplace depends mainly on two variables:

- The degree of similarity between what they learned in the training session (including how it was presented) and what occurs in the workplace (for example, Can trainees apply their new knowledge and skills directly to the job without modifying them?)

- The degree to which trainees can integrate the skills and knowledge gained in the training session into their work environment (for example, Does the system at work or the supervisor allow or encourage using the new skills?).

Make sure to consider these variables as you plan your training program. Make three-by-five cards that define the lesson and the outcome objective. These cards are tools that trainees can take with them to use as references back on the job. Develop a checklist of all the learning outcomes for the training. Have learners check off each outcome as they perform them when they are on the job. Either provide each learner with a journal to use to record his or her progress after the training, or check with each learner approximately one month after the training to get feedback on the training transfer.

Incorporate Instructional Elements

When designing the training session, trainers should address the following 10 instructional elements: expectations, measurement, capacity, prerequisites, attitudes and motivation, instruction, instructional resources, feedback, motivational climate (potential for leadership and inspiration), and performance support. Following is an explanation of how each can strengthen the training sessions:

Expectations

Clarifying expectations, learning objectives, or learning goals is key to designing the training session. From the beginning, trainees must understand the desired outcome of the training and the relationship between those outcomes and their jobs. It is not sufficient to define the learning objectives as part of your introduction. Throughout the session you must reiterate the objectives that you have integrated into the session design. By adhering to the following guidelines in your consideration of expectations, you will be well on your way to designing successful training sessions.

- Write clearly and directly.

- Explain the reason or reasons for the training.

- Relate the training to work performance.

- Clarify management's role.

- Negotiate and discuss with trainees to gain their ownership of the training.
- Review regularly and revise if necessary.

Measurement

Expectations are more likely to be met fully if the training design incorporates the means by which the trainer, trainees, and management can measure progress toward accomplishing them. Incorporate the following elements into the design:

- measurable training objectives
- measurable performance requirements aligned with training requirements
- methods that do not threaten trainees
- methods that allow for self- or peer measurement.

Capacity

Successful training can occur only if trainees have the capacities to succeed. Trainers should take care to do the following:

- Identify capacity requirements for training and job performance.
- Screen prospective trainees for physical, intellectual, or emotional capacity prior to their selection as part of the group.
- Provide opportunities for remedial training whenever possible and appropriate for trainees who do not meet certain capacity requirements.

Prerequisites

After taking the above steps to ensure that trainees have the capacity to do the job for which the training is being designed, you may find that some trainees lack certain skills and the requisite knowledge base. Failure to address these gaps when designing the session would not be fair either to the trainees with the deficits or to those with the requisite skills and knowledge base. Consider taking the following steps:

- Specify clearly and in advance the prerequisites for the training.
- Study the trainees' characteristics.
- Administer pretests whenever possible and appropriate.

- Ask questions randomly to determine the trainees' general level of preparation.
- Design the training to meet the group's preparation level (aim at the middle; see chapter six, "Implementation").
- Prepare alternative routes through the course of instruction on the basis of the group's preparation level.

Attitudes and Motivation

Trainees must have positive attitudes and be motivated to benefit from training. As a trainer, you can increase the likelihood that trainees will have positive attitudes in the following ways:

- Do what you can to ensure that trainees are informed well in advance about the forthcoming training session.
- Exclude threatening or competitive issues from your materials and content.
- Include input from the trainees and union leadership (if relevant) in the design.
- Relate training to job requirements.
- Encourage prospective trainees to volunteer to attend.
- Build adequate amenities, such as beverages, lunch, and food for breaks, into the program. (You don't have to provide amenities equal to those from a luxury spa, but trainees should not feel as if they are in boot camp.)

Instruction

Although the design of instructional materials is extremely important to successful training, materials cannot substitute for high-quality instruction. By adhering to the following guidelines, trainers can ensure that their instruction will be top notch:

- Involve the entire trainee population in icebreakers and a discussion of their expectations.
- Demonstrate the skills or the learning that is to be trained.
- Provide brief and to-the-point content.
- Encourage feedback at every step.

- Build in several opportunities for trainees to practice.
- Pace the training to the trainees' level.
- Allow significant time for questions and answers.

Instructional Resources

Remember that you are training people to perform in their regular work settings. The training you provide must, therefore, be easy for them to transfer from your session and replicate on their jobs. Trainees who lack appropriate resources when they return to their work settings will not be able to replicate what they have learned. Understanding that this may be the case, you need to know what resources trainees will have available to them before you design the training session. Be sure to do the following:

- Request an inventory of resources.
- Conduct an inventory of resources if none is available.
- Incorporate the resources into the training design.
- Identify as many as possible of the following instructional resources:
  — access to follow-up information
  — reference materials
  — allocated time to practice what was taught
  — individuals assigned to help trainees apply what they learned
  — support materials, such as training videos.

Feedback

Feedback is critical to the success of any type of intervention. Trainees need to receive clear, appropriate, and timely information about their performance both in the training session and on the job. Feedback systems should be designed to provide trainees with performance-based information that specifically takes into account what they have learned in training, especially during the first several weeks following the training session. Three types of feedback are especially important:

- trainer's feedback, in staff and team meetings
- supervisor's positive feedback
- peer trainees' corrective feedback, provided it is given with sensitivity.

Remind all those involved feedback must be based on specific information that the person receiving the feedback understands and on performance that the person can apply.

Motivational Climate

As mentioned earlier, positive attitudes and motivation are critical to effective training and performance. To a large extent, motivational climate determines whether attitudes are positive or negative and the direction and strength of motivation. Determine if any factors are adversely affecting learning and performance and, if they are, correct the problems by doing the following:

- removing constraints and barriers to learning and performance

- ensuring that positive consequences follow positive performance

- ensuring that negative consequences do not follow positive performance

- developing a supportive, trusting environment for learning and performance

- providing opportunities for participation

- increasing follow through on employee suggestions.

Performance Support

Frequently the link between training and on-the-job performance is tenuous or totally neglected. To support performance once trainees have returned to work, suggest to management they consider implementing the following actions:

- Hold follow-up meetings that include trainees.

- Provide trainees with adequate opportunities to use their new skills and knowledge.

- Reinforce what trainees learned.

- Empower trainees to explore new areas.

- Allow trainees to fail at new endeavors without penalizing them.

- Integrate supervisors into the training process.

TYPES OF TRAINING DESIGN

Two general types of design, which may be viewed on a continuum, are available. At one end is a totally preplanned design, and at the other is an emerging design.

In a preplanned design, the trainer decides everything in advance for each session. Of course, be open to the reality that you may need to alter, rearrange, add, or drop your plans. However, understand that to design successful training programs, you must adhere to the goals, techniques, and evaluation criteria that you established in advance. The new or relatively inexperienced trainer should use preplanned design.

Below are some guidelines for preplanned design:

- Avoid overplanning, especially minute-by-minute outlines.

- Allow for flexibility.

- Prepare for some resistance to change if feedback during the training indicates the need to make changes.

In an emerging design, little is decided in advance. By designing at the moment, the trainer maximizes the effect of the trainees' experiences and interactions on the training activity. Sometimes an emerging design will have a plan only for the opening session, with the remainder of the plans emerging as the training proceeds. An emerging design requires minimal preplanning and maximum trainer's skills.

Following are some guidelines for emerging designs:

- Advertise the training activity accurately so that trainees will know that a flexible design will be used.

- Adhere to the design.

- Stop occasionally during the training to ask yourself, "Is this producing learning in accordance with our goals?"

Whatever design you use, remember that adult learners absorb material best when it is given during presentations, demonstrations, readings, dramas, discussions, case studies, visual aids, role plays, games, and participant-directed inquiries.

Adult Learner Styles

Adult learners bring rich life experiences to your training. Here are some general principles to consider in your design process to facilitate learning for adults. Members of this group:

- make their own decisions about which aspects of the training are important
- validate the information presented based on their specific beliefs and experiences
- have a lot of experience and have fixed viewpoints
- bring significant knowledge to the training
- expect what they learn to be useful immediately.

During their formal education process, many adult learners found that they could best learn and use the information by a certain kind of instructor. Let's consider trainer styles, an important ingredient in the design process.

TRAINER STYLES

There are three trainer styles: authoritarian, laissez-faire, and democratic. Each style affects the learning process. At one extreme is the authoritarian style, which tends to dominate the learning process by having the information flow be a one-way process from the trainer to the learner. This style leaves little room for learners to interact with the trainer. In training, the authoritarian style of communication limits learning.

At the other extreme is the laissez-faire style. It may lead the learners to feel that there is too little direction and that the learning experience is disorganized and not well planned. The trainer might establish the focus of the conversation or topic, for example, and then turn the dialogue over to the trainees for them to manage the direction, content, and flow of the exchange. Using the laissez-faire style of communication in training may confuse learning.

The democratic style offers a more balanced approach. The trainer establishes an in-session dialogue with the trainees. Both the trainer and trainees have equal responsibility to promote the topic. This approach allows for the interplay of personalities among the trainer and the learners. With the democratic style of communication in the training, the instructional foundation is solid and learning is collaborative.

SUMMARY AND HIGHLIGHTS

Learning objectives are the most important element in the design and development process. The learning objectives define the topic, the content, and, to some degree, the learning and teaching process.

There are three essential components when developing an objective:

- the performance statement, which means the action or behavior the learner must exhibit after the training event
- the condition, which means the tools, equipment, or document necessary to be used in the learning process
- criteria, which is the level of standard that the learner's performance must meet.

Organize and design the content you are to teach with the five learner styles in mind. The five styles are

- the confident learner, who likes to be involved and consulted
- the affective (feeling) learner
- the transitional learner, who is making a job change and wants the learning to apply in the new situation
- the risk taker, who thrives on new information and skills.

The acronym *LEARN* defines the essential design guidelines involving adult learning. These are

- *L* for learner directed
- *E,* experiential
- *A,* able to be evaluated
- *R,* residual
- *N,* numerous instructional methods.

These steps define the adult learning principles that provide the framework for organizing the learning process. These principles ensure that your design will be structured so that adult learners can participate in the learning process and not feel anxious about events that will happen during the learning process.

Establish and design your training design format using the 10 instructional elements. They are the tools you need for organizing your topic and program structure. Putting them to work requires that you do the following:

- Clarify expectations.
- Develop an outcome measurement mechanism.
- Cluster content around the learners' capacity.
- Provide prerequisites when you present new information.
- Take steps to ensure that trainees had positive attitudes.
- Follow guidelines to high-quality instruction.
- Identify instructional resources for further mastery beyond the training.
- Provide feedback.
- Assess motivational climate.
- Integrate adult learning principles in your design and delivery strategies.

Development

INTRODUCTION

Development is the process of creating, testing, and producing usable instructional materials. You have defined the topic to be developed by creating your learning objectives and establishing your topic content.

Throughout the development process, training team members—the group of people you've selected to work with you—who are knowledgeable in the content area, instructional design, and evaluation, continually review the major training materials in development. They review the revisions and use pilot testing to check program material prior to delivery of the formal training program.

The choice of an appropriate instructional strategy for a particular audience is, at best, a guess if you have not been able to conduct a formal audience needs analysis. One way to avoid mismatching an instructional strategy with a particular audience is to be sensitive to an organization's demographics and preferences. In all cases, the word that guides your choice is *appropriate* use of instructional technology. The technology should be suitable for the audience, the content, the organizational environment, and, most of all, the proposed learning objective. These preferences provide you with:

- a design template to assist in developing the content of your course material
- a checklist for making decisions about learning activities.

What is meant by instruction and instructional strategies? The central purpose of any training or educational intervention or program is to promote learning. Instruction promotes learning through a set of events developed to initiate, activate, and support learning.

Use instructional strategies to:

- motivate learners
- help learners prepare for learning
- enable learners to apply and practice learning
- assist learners to retain and transfer what they have learned
- integrate your own performance with other skills and knowledge.

Instructional strategies, sometimes called presentation strategies, are the mechanisms through which instruction is presented. The most common strategies are:

- *Lecture:* The course instructor presents the content of the course. Communication is primarily one-way, from the instructor to the learner.
- *Role-play:* Participants assume roles and act out situations that they play spontaneously to emphasize concepts presented.
- *Group discussion:* Class members discuss a given topic. Ideas are accepted from all participants.
- *Self-discovery:* Learners discover the content of the course on their own by using a variety of techniques, such as research and guided exercises.
- *Self-paced/programmed instruction:* Learners read or perform course-related activities, progressing through the program at their own pace.
- *Case studies:* Learners analyze situations and draw conclusions or recommend solutions on the basis of the content presented in the course.
- *Competitive games:* Learners compete against one another in teams or as individuals in a fun-based activity where one team or individual is the winner.
- *Cooperative games:* Learners work together in teams or as individuals in a fun-based activity to reach a common goal in which all teams or individuals win.

- *Movies/videos:* Content comes primarily from movies or video-tapes.
- *Individual projects:* Learners work individually to apply the concepts present in the course.
- *Group projects:* Learners work in teams to apply the concepts present in the course.
- *Simulation:* Learners participate in a reality-based, interactive activity that imitates a more complex simulation in order to facilitate learning.

SELECTING INSTRUCTIONAL STRATEGIES

The appropriate strategy to use for a presentation depends on a variety of factors, including the following:

- type of learning (verbal information, intellectual skills, cognitive strategy, attitude, or motor skill)
- audience
- demographics or profile (including age, gender, level of education)
- learning styles (for example, kinsethetic-tactile, visual, auditory)
- number of learners (individual, small groups, large groups, and the like)
- media (selected by appropriateness, number of learners, and financial considerations)
- budget (funds available for development as well as presentation)
- physical site (centralized, decentralized, specialized)
- instructor's skills and training style.

Each factor, in combination with the others, influences the choice of a strategy for presenting, reinforcing, and assessing the retention of the material. A model depicting the relationship among these factors is shown in figure 1.

LEARNING PREFERENCES

People who are motivated learn. As you develop your intervention, assume that the audience is more likely to participate when the material is

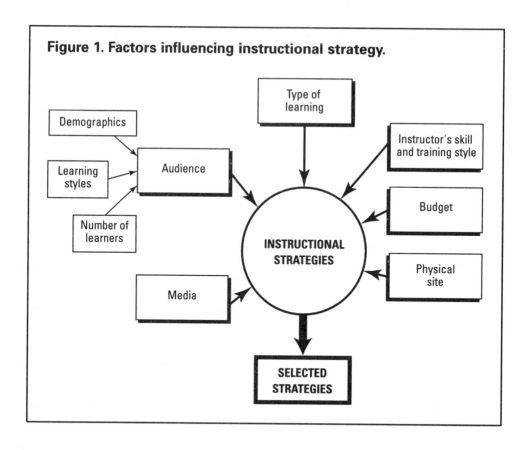

Figure 1. Factors influencing instructional strategy.

presented in a relaxed, informal learning environment that is conducive to trainees' and the trainer's interaction. A learning environment that is relaxed but structured—with an agenda, objectives, and established time frames and tasks—is one in which participants will be willing to participate and, therefore, is one in which the learning will be successful. There is a relationship between the target audience's demographics and their preferences for particular instructional strategies. A conducive learning environment leads to:

- increased attention and motivation
- increased mastery
- more successful transfer of what's been learned back to the learner's own environment
- enhanced retention and recall.

By understanding the trainees' profiles and demographics, you are more likely to be sensitive to the different instructional strategies they prefer. In most cases, during your analysis and design process, you have only basic information about the target audience, including:

- age (usually a range)
- gender
- occupation (current as well as previous on occasion)
- race or ethnic group (known only occasionally because of Equal Employment Opportunity Commission considerations)
- years of work experience (usually a range).

The demographics alone do not reveal a learner's preference, although this information is a good starting place. Group discussions tend to be one of the training methods people like most, followed by case studies, games, and role playing. Lectures and telecommunication methods such TV lectures are two of the methods people like least. Videotapes and films, intrapersonal and interpersonal training, and self-instruction and computer-based instruction fall in the middle. By discovering which instructional strategies different groups prefer, you are better able to develop and deliver training that specific audiences like and consider motivating.

In the 1970s, David McClelland, a psychologist with the Boston-based management consulting firm McBer and Associates, used the works of Carl Jung to identify predominant learning styles. This researcher asserted that there are three main learning style preferences:

- Hepatic learners, also called kinesthetic-tactile learners, learn best when they are involved, moving, experiencing, and experimenting.
- Visual learners learn best when they see pictures of what they are studying. A small percentage are print-oriented and learn best by reading.
- Auditory learners learn best through sound, such as music and talk.

MOTIVATING LEARNERS

Responding to adult learners' preferences for one instructional strategy over another can help you to improve their motivation to learn. Success, volition, value, and enjoyment create a motivated learner. When you develop your material, you can enhance motivation by relating learning to age-specific adult interests and using relevant topics to set the stage regardless of the specific instructional design. To quote Richard Boyatzis (1982), Case Western Reserve University, "That which excites, stimulates, challenges, bores, or annoys us is determined, in large part, by our life and career stages." One way to reach trainees of different stages during a session is to use a variety of examples. An example about being a parent, for example, would not be helpful to trainees who had no children.

A Word to the Wise

In an interview that a class I taught in 1993 conducted of Leonard Nadler, the father of the field of human resource development, he spoke about the importance of collecting and using demographic information to guide instruction and select instructional strategies. He said, "...I always encouraged instructional designers and developers to collect and review data about the particular group they are to train since no group ever has the same characteristics and preconceptions based on overgeneralizations from prior analyses."

Given this cautionary note, Nadler stated that the first question trainers must ask is whether they are focusing on education (learning provided to improve performance on a future job, which typically means theory) or training (learning that is provided to improve performance on the present job, which typically means skills training). If the answer is education, then the most important question to answer before finalizing the training intervention is, What has been the previous success or failure of the learners in educational settings. If the answer is training, then you look at skills.

CONSTRUCTING A TRAINING PROGRAM

The instructional specifications serve as a blueprint for program development because they determine what content to include, when to include it, and why. They also serve as a foundation for evaluation activities.

Course design is linked to course development through a series of documents, which include the profiles described in the last chapter. From these documents, you create your initial blueprint. The blueprint should list the course objectives. Supportive information about the subject matter or course content should then be linked to each objective. You also may want to identify which objectives are to be met in the training presentation and which apply to the workplace.

Technique for Specifying Strategies

Training and content experts together select the instructional content. They systematically define the critical content components or modules and show how the instructional strategies will be used to introduce content. In addition, they determine appropriate learning techniques, develop opportunities for practice, and select appropriate media. Remember, all the media should have a definite purpose; you choose them to amplify learning, not to entertain a bored audience.

The instructional specifications include:

- module name
- introduction (content summary, utility, importance)
- sequence of topics and activities (flow, transitions, links).

For each objective, there should be documentation elaborating the following:

- special teaching points
- instructional methods to be used
- media requirements
- testing requirements.

Designing the Sequence and Strategies

You should develop the training sequence in a logical order. Frequently, more than one logical order may be an appropriate way for learning a task. You must choose the sequencing method most suited to the learning tasks and demographics of the group members.

The usual sequences are step by step, simple to complex, or overview to detailed learning. Step by step is a good choice if a task is always done in a certain order. Simple to complex is better when it's appropriate to have learners develop simple skills first, and then build on them to learn more complex skills. When it's appropriate for learners to know how an entire system or process works before they learn its separate tasks, they should get an overview before detailed learning.

At this point, select the overall training intervention strategies. Details can be worked out when specific materials are chosen. For now, make general decisions about the training method or methods and the training media. Ask yourself, Will the course include on-the-job training, classroom instruction, lab or workshop instruction, or self-instruction?

Will the course use textbooks, consumable workbooks, computers, interactive videodisks, or audiotapes or videotapes?

The strategies you select must match the stated objectives of the course or intervention. For example, the strategies for a course to help trainees master computer skills should not rely heavily on pencil and paper activities. Participants would need opportunities for hands-on computer practice in order to pass a job-related evaluation at the course's end.

Developing Test Items

The second step in developing instructional strategies is to design test items to be used during the training intervention to check on the progress of learning. Well-written objectives call for a learner to demonstrate observable, measurable actions. Objectives shouldn't include verbs like *understand* or *know* because they describe a learner's internal state, which cannot be observed.

Ask yourself if the objective statement is really a test of the learner's ability to describe work or of the person's ability to do work. By looking at objectives in terms of how they will be tested, you may want to identify subordinate (but still important) skills and knowledge that were overlooked during the task analysis. Your main task is to identify and correct poor objectives before training materials are developed to support them.

The objective statement should be a well-defined outcome. Once the outcome or objective statement is defined, it serves as the master blueprint for designing the course and module development as well as the supporting instructional and participant materials. However, this degree of detail is often lacking in course objectives. Moreover, course objectives may not be an effective set of documents to communicate outcomes to your client, but the end-of-course criterion test would be.

The criterion test is another part of the blueprint that will help you develop the training course. If the training course or intervention is long enough to warrant intermediate mastery tests, you should specify the behaviors to be measured at each checkpoint, along with any suggestions on the format of the test. You should place whatever format you select for the blueprint in a reference binder for subsequent use by the following people:

- the course developer or developers and suppliers in specialized media

- the instructor or instructors to get an overview of the content of the course
- the training department staff, to be able to counsel employees on which course to take
- the managers, to determine if a course contains specific material for themselves or their staff.

Identification of Support Requirements

Support requirements include materials, equipment, and administrative support. They include computers, flipcharts, and other logistical support you need to design, develop, implement, and evaluate the training program or course. It is critical to identify support requirements to ensure that necessary support resources will be available when you need them.

Technique for Establishing Training Design Requirement

When you have the objectives and the media requirements, you can estimate the support resources you'll need and the number of days the training program should last.

The list in table 1 identifies some of the typical items necessary for running a training program. Itemized lists like this can help trainers make sure that they've arranged all the support personnel and materials they need for their programs.

Analysis Outputs

Having completed the task analysis, written the objectives, and designed test items, you now have a good idea of what is going to be included in the training program. The next step for many people is to outline the information and develop a course map, which identifies all the steps that lead to completion of the course. Some people develop the course map as soon as they have completed the job and task analysis, whereas others wait until they have begun to develop the course materials and instructional strategies. Either way, it is critical to keep your audience and the purpose of the course in mind as you develop it.

The course map lists in hierarchical order the modules within units, as figure 2 shows. Some trainers describe the hierarchy as modules within chapters or as units within lessons within modules. The terminology is not important.

Table 1. Support requirements checklist.			
ITEM	**DATE REQUIRED**	**DATE ORDERED**	**COST (IF APPLICABLE)**
Travel and lodging (T&L) costs			
T&L arrangements			
Consultant fees			
Graphics			
Reproduction (notebooks, CBT, job aids)			
Documentation production schedule			
Materials (e.g., tabs, binders)			
Compile binders			
Gifts, prizes, mementos			
Temporary personnel			
Facility availability			
Equipment availability			
Evaluation forms			
Media arrangements			
Instructor scheduling			
Instructor training			
Software costs			
Software reproduction			
Software distribution			
Legal review			

Source: McArdle, Geri, Training Systems Institute, Reston, VA. 1995.

This map is accompanied by media selections and support requirements. (Note: The analogous map for computer-based training (CBT) may be a skeleton storyboard, which shows frame by frame what will appear in the computer training.)

You should think about these influences on your course as you design the course map and ensure that the design is consistent with them:

- course objectives
- class size
- training site
- pre- and postcourse work

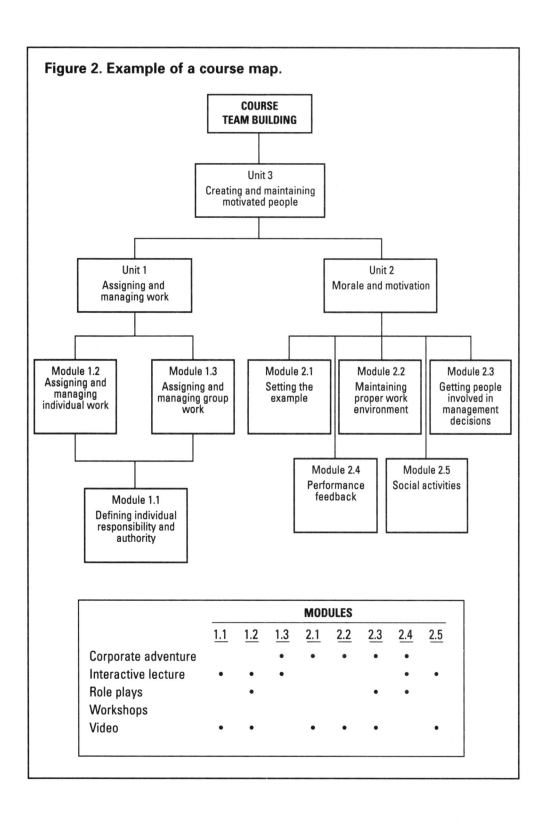

Figure 2. Example of a course map.

COURSE
TEAM BUILDING

Unit 3
Creating and maintaining
motivated people

Unit 1
Assigning and
managing work

Unit 2
Morale and motivation

Module 1.2
Assigning and
managing
individual work

Module 1.3
Assigning and
managing group
work

Module 2.1
Setting the
example

Module 2.2
Maintaining
proper work
environment

Module 2.3
Getting people
involved in
management
decisions

Module 2.4
Performance
feedback

Module 2.5
Social activities

Module 1.1
Defining individual
responsibility and
authority

| | | MODULES | | | | | |
	1.1	1.2	1.3	2.1	2.2	2.3	2.4	2.5
Corporate adventure			•	•	•	•	•	
Interactive lecture	•	•	•				•	•
Role plays		•				•	•	
Workshops								
Video	•	•		•	•	•		•

- course materials
- delivery strategy and instructor needs
- multilevel audience experience
- course relationship to job conditions
- learner motivation and accountability.

It is important to consider the big picture when you develop a course or program. Once you have identified the reasons for the course, your next step is to develop a course or program sequence. Here are some guidelines for sequencing the entire course:

- Focus on what happens on the job.
- Use the job analysis to establish the sequence of chapters.
- Arrange the course in sequence from general to specific, from simple to complex.
- When there is no job-related basis for sequencing, arrange the course in the most logical fashion for the learner.
- If a model for performance is available, such as a problem-solving or a training design model, use it as a guide for sequencing.
- Use the same training advisory group to test the sequence as you did to validate other areas of your analysis and design process.

Modules

Adult learners respond best to small organized units of learning, so organize the course content into modules. (Sometimes the term *lesson* refers to these distinct units of content.) A module is the smallest unit of learning and provides content and practice on the basis of predefined learning objectives. Each module relates to a specific task in the task analysis, so that at the end of the training, the learner should be able to perform the task.

Let's consider a course in problem analysis. You have created your objectives, your test items, and your topic content. You are now ready to develop a course and module map. The first thing you do is list all of the elements that you consider necessary to teach. Next, you organize them in a logical framework, and then you develop subtopics.

Here is an example of a course and module design for program analysis that Rosemary Brehm put together for me. (Rosemary Brehm, of the training firm Partners in Training, in Tampa, Florida, teaches the course Instructional Design Course for Trainers with me for the American Management Association.)

Chapter 1: Problem Analysis
    Module 1: How to state the problem
    Module 2: How to define the standard
    Module 3: How to define the difference

Chapter 2: Cause Identification
    Module 1: How to determine training deficiencies
    Module 2: How to determine other deficiencies

Chapter 3: Data Collection
    Module 1: How to create data collection questions
    Module 2: How to use data collection sources
    Module 3: How to manage data collection

Chapter 4: Idea Generation
    Module 1: How to use individual techniques
    Module 2: How to use group techniques

Chapter 5: Solution Selection
    Module 1: How to evaluate ideas
    Module 2: How to select best idea

Chapter 6: Solution Implementation
    Module 1: How to manage resources
    Module 2: How to complete a time and action plan

Chapter 7: Solution Evaluation
    Module 1: How to measure impact of solution
    Module 2: How to document results

Each learning module contains the following:

- objectives
- knowledge content to enable the learner to complete the task
- task content
- practice activities to help reach the objective or objectives

- an assessment mechanism such as a test item to determine if the objective or objectives were achieved.

Other factors to take into account when creating the module include:

- best method to use to get objective across
- timing and breaks
- amount of material to cover
- class size; group size for activities
- simulation of job conditions.

The module design serves as a major section of your course blueprint for developing the content and instructional strategies (see table 2). To create a module, consider the following elements in each module you design:

- State the objective.
- Identify content topics.

Table 2. Sample module design.

MODULE NAME:_____

OBJECTIVE	CONTENT	INSTRUCTOR AND LEARNER ACTIVITIES

- Identify trainer and learner activities that will result in mastery of the objective, including methods and media used by trainer and learner.

DESIGN REPORT

The design report is a summary of the analysis and design completed to date. It serves as a preliminary communiqué to inform management of your progress and provides an opportunity for suggestions and feedback. It is a way to ensure that training meets management's expectations because managers' support for your training objectives and course outcomes is critical to your success as well as the success of your program and the trainees.

The report serves to inform management of the proposed training intervention, it provides a so-called road map for the instructional designer to use in developing the training intervention, and it provides the course instructor with background information with respect to how and why the training intervention was developed.

A design report contains several narrative components:

- purpose of the course
- summary of the analysis
- scope of the course
- test item strategy
- course and module design
- delivery strategy
- level of evaluation to be tested.

The following Problem-Solving Course for New Managers is a sample design report.

PROBLEM-SOLVING COURSE FOR NEW MANAGERS

Purpose of the Course *page 1*

The course will introduce new managers to the established problem-solving strategies developed at our company. These problem-solving skills will be separated into sessions. The course will integrate current company issues into the program, rather than use issues discussed when the course was last held five years ago.

Summary of Analyses

Needs analysis and problem analysis: When the course was last given, these analyses led to the development of an internal problem-solving model for use during management sessions. That model was successful, but it needs updating.

Audience analysis: The company has 30 managers located in eight different regions who need to learn the problem-solving model to participate more effectively in management meetings.

Job and task analysis: The problem-solving model already exists. We need to customize it to meet the new managers' needs and overcome questions about our new product line. Attached is our survey of their needs.

Scope of the Course

This course will use a seven-stage model of problem solving. The three-day course will be held at our corporate headquarters. All new managers will attend.

Task Learning Objective   *page 2*

Objective 1: Given the problem-solving model and one case-study scenario, resolve the customer question to the level of satisfaction of the instruction.

Objective 2: Given the product features guidelines and the problem-solving model, resolve the customer product complaint to the satisfaction of the customer within acceptable guidelines of the company policy.

Objective 3: List and define the steps in the problem-solving model.

Item Strategy

The learners will have to demonstrate mastery of the problem-solving model by using all seven stages of the model in two case studies in the workshop. They will be assessed at the end of each chapter.

Course and Module Plans

Attached are detailed course and module plans.

Course and Module Plan

Objectives   Content

Activities

Delivery Strategy   *page 3*

This workshop will be an instructor-led, three-day classroom training session. The instructor team will include a member of the training staff and an experienced company manager.

The course will be held at corporate headquarters.

Evaluation Stages Measured

Stage 1: Learner Reaction Stage. Daily classroom reaction sheets.

Stage 2: Learning. Test items will measure learning.

Stage 3: Behavior. Surveys will be sent to all management before and after training to assess changes in managerial problem solving.

WRITING LESSON PLANS

Once you've completed your course and module design, your next step is to develop a lesson, or session, plan. The set of detailed notes that you write will guide you through the material development and delivery processes. The elements of a lesson should include the following:

- session title
- learning objectives
- timing
- key learning points
- brief content synopsis
- presentation methodology
- definition of terms

- key questions to ask
- resource requirements
- learner activities
- topic transitions
- review checks
- learner issues.

The format of the suggested lesson plan, shown in table 3, includes five columns: timing, content, training techniques, trainee activity, and training aids. Following is a description of each item:

Table 3. Format of a lesson plan.				
TIMING	CONTENT (WHAT TO BE TAUGHT)	TRAINING TECHNIQUES	TRAINEE ACTIVITY	TRAINING AIDS

- Under timing in the table, list the time you will spend on each topic and subtopic of each session. A typical training day is six hours, and you have 55 minutes in an hour for training. You should provide at least 10 percent of the time to introduce or make a transition to the topic, and devote 70 percent of your time to content delivery, which might include preparing the learner to learn (stating the objective), presenting the material, and practicing using the material with an exercise and feedback. The final 20 percent of the time should be devoted to summary, conclusion, and transition to the next lesson or module.

- Under content, list the topic and subtopics that you will cover during each session. Do not combine sessions. Develop and deliver each session topic independently, using transitional statements to bridge from one topic or subtopic to another. In the session plan, indicate introductions, breaks, and sequences in one session. Don't have "run-on" sessions without using transition statements. Run-on sessions are those that continue after a lunch or other break or even from one day to the next. Deliver your content in complete and inclusive parts. Illogical breaks that occur because trainers did not scope the content appropriately leave the trainer in an awkward situation and the learning incomplete.

- The training technique column is for explaining in basic terms whether the session is to be a lecture, show and tell, or perhaps participant discovery.

- Under trainees' activity, you should list the types of things that the learner will be doing during the session (listening, looking, practicing, and so forth). By documenting this information, you'll have the opportunity to build a variety of activities into your training course in advance.

- In the training aids column, list the instructional aids and strategies or peripherals that you'll use and the order in which you'll use them.

As you begin to write your plan, ask yourself two questions, What is the purpose of this training presentation? and What do learners need to know?

Too much information at one time creates confusion. *Chunking* is the term for breaking down concepts into meaningful parts. Give a learner a maximum of three large pieces of information. In a module, if you have three major components to the topic, deliver them within an hour. Once you deliver the three large chunks within an hour, it's time to summarize and break.

Cluster the topical information that you have researched in organized sections, such as introduction, body, and activities. Next, use the technique of "grading the content" to target the correct amount of information to deliver. Figure 3 shows a simple way of grading, or targeting, the material you'll deliver.

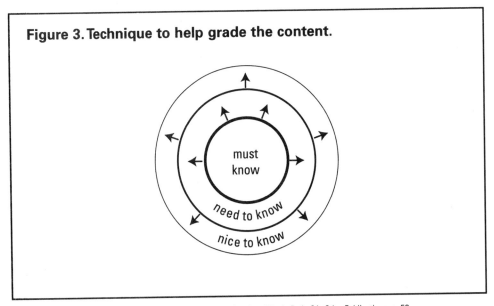

Figure 3. Technique to help grade the content.

Source: McArdle, G.E.H. (1993). *Delivering Effective Training Sessions.* Menlo Park, CA: Crisp Publications, p. 59.

The "must know" information is the enabling knowledge that the learner needs to know to perform the task or job. The "need to know" information may be needed for the learner to gain a clear understanding of the essential information presented during the session. The "nice to know" information encompasses items that are not necessary to know and might illustrate the points covered in the session.

It's reasonable for you to assume that if you develop your instruction at the bull's eye, the "must know" area, a certain amount of time also would be spent in the "need to know" area as a review. If time permits, let the learners look at the "nice to know" area, but the time would probably be better spent reviewing the "need to know" and "must know" areas. You must deliver too little well, rather than too much badly.

Lesson Plans Are "Look Aheads"

A lesson plan allows you to determine in advance if the delivery sequence is correct, the content is relevant to the topic and the learner, and your instructional strategies are appropriate. The lesson plan also acts as a resource checklist. It allows you to prepare for any information or material that may be required for the lesson, such as handouts, overheads, video-tapes, flipcharts, and wall charts. The essential elements in the lesson plan are timing, learning objectives, brief summaries of each topic point, learner and trainer activities, and needed materials. The structure of the session plan should be a format that you feel comfortable using. An example of a lesson plan appears in table 4.

(Caution: Do not make your lesson plan too elaborate or complicated. The lesson plan is a road map, your course map, to help you organize your course, from the beginning through the end. By referring to it as you present your program, you may find it assists your delivery as well.)

INSTRUCTIONAL RESOURCES

During the development phase, you select, write, or otherwise obtain all training, documentation, and evaluation materials. These may include the following:

- training materials
- instructor guide (including lesson plans and a list of required supporting materials)
- trainees' guides or workbooks
- nonprint media (computer software, audiotapes and videotapes, equipment checklists)
- program evaluation materials
- procedures for training program evaluations
- course evaluation forms

- supervisors' forms for evaluation of course participants' post-training job performance
- training documentation
- class attendance forms and other records for training participants
- course documentation (written objectives, authorship and responsibility for course material, lists of instructors and facilitators, and their qualifications).

DEVELOPMENT OUTPUTS

The output of the development stage is a training program that is ready to be implemented. The development process consists of five phases,

---

Table 4. Sample lesson plan.

TITLE:	How to use the bundling machine
WRITTEN BY:	Author's Name **DATE:** Date Written
OBJECTIVES:	At the end of this session, the participants will be able to: 1. State one reason for using the bundling machine 2. Demonstrate the correct use of the bundling machine located in the workshop 3. State when the bundling machine is used
SESSION TIME:	15 minutes
NUMBER OF PARTICIPANTS:	6 (up to 10)
ENTRY LEVEL:	New employees
AIDS/EQUIPMENT:	Sample bundling machine 6 bundling cards for each participant whiteboard and markers
POTENTIAL FAULTS:	Session not to be conducted at start or finish time of workshop
METHOD:	Show and tell

(Table 4 *continued*)

TIMING (MINUTES)	CONTENT (WHAT TO BE TAUGHT)	TRAINING TECHNIQUES	TRAINEE ACTIVITY	TRAINING AIDS
Intro 0-2	Introduction: – topic – facilitator Link back to previous session Motivator – pay requirement	Lecture	Listening	W/board
Body 2-10	Describe bundling machine and purpose	Lecture	Listening	Sample machine and card
	How to use machine	Show and tell	Observation	Sample machine and card
	How to fix simple problems	Show and tell	Observation	Sample machine
		Go to work-shop	Practice	Machine and cards
Conclusion 10-15	Each participant to demon-strate hands-on correct use of the bundling in the work-shop	Hands-on	Doing/test	Machine and cards
	Questions to group: – Give one reason for using the bundling – When do you use the bundling?	Questions	Answering verbally	
	Link to next session on pay and conditions			

Source: Used with permission from Kroehnert, Gary. (1994). *Basic Training for Trainers, Revised Edition*. Sample Session Plan, pages 60–61. Sydney, Australia: McGraw-Hill Book Company.

each one of which leads to the next. Following is a description of the phases:

- Phase one: Develop the following:
    - training program content
    - graphics
    - media needs
    - lesson plans
    - instructor guides
    - evaluation needs

— software needs.

— Review the materials developed.

- Phase two: Revise the following:
  — training program content
  — graphics
  — media needs
  — lesson plans
  — instructor guides
  — evaluation needs
  — software needs.
  — Review the revised material.

- Phase three, do the following:
  — Conduct the test.
  — Revise the program on the basis of the test.
  — Schedule a second test if needed.

- Phase four, do the following:
  — Pilot test a prototype program.
  — Evaluate the pilot test.
  — Identify the required revisions.
  — Revise the program as required (on the basis of the pilot test).
  — Schedule a second test if needed.

- Phase five, do the following:
  — Finalize the training program content.
  — Produce the training program in final form.

TRAINING MATERIALS

Training materials must support course objectives. Resources may be ready-made materials chosen for a specific course, customized materials designed for a specific course or module, materials taken from a previous course developed in-house, or new materials purchased from outside vendors.

Off-the-shelf materials save development time. However, my experience with off-the-shelf material is that the topic or content is generic, which means it can appeal to any audience. If you need the material you present to be customer focused, then you'll have to spend time and resources customizing it.

Make sure that you keep a library of all course materials that you use. It just might be that on occasion, you could use a predesigned module from an in-house customized course that would fit well with a new course you develop. That's okay. The material belongs to your company. It's better to have customized material than generic material in your training programs. You have more control of the content and the rationale for the designed components of the training.

Program Evaluation Materials

Evaluation forms should be easy to understand and require a minimum of time to complete. Plans should be made to ensure that they are complete and that they get collected, otherwise you'll get incomplete, possibly invalid, information.

Once an evaluation is completed on a course, it's necessary to provide copies of the evaluations to the course developer, the course evaluator, and the course administrator. Each one of these key individuals evaluates the content of the evaluation remarks differently and acts on the content. For example, the developer looks for evaluative remarks concerning the topic treatment and the instructional events. These data will serve as the basis for course revisions.

Training Documentation Materials

Training records can be kept in paper files or on a computer. To maintain training records, try Registrar or other record-keeping software. The course administrator can be responsible for maintaining the database.

LEGAL IMPLICATIONS

Since the 1960s, a number of federal laws have been passed that require employers to provide equal opportunity in employment and career progression. All of these laws require employers to inform employees of their rights through positing and notices by posting the laws, related notices, and position openings. You should be familiar with the following laws that affect training and development.

Title VII, Civil Rights Act

Congress passed Title VII of the Civil Rights Act of 1964 to bring about equality in hiring, transfers, promotions, access to training, and other employment-related decisions. Title VII also stipulated that there must be equal opportunity to participate in training programs. If employees have nondiscriminatory access to the same training, everyone will have the opportunity to be better qualified for advancement.

Age Discrimination in Employment Act (1967)

The Age Discrimination in Employment Act (ADEA) was enacted in 1967 to protect older workers. Generally, the ADEA protects workers over the age of 40 against employment discrimination on the basis of age. This protection includes giving qualified employees over 40 years of age equal accessibility to training.

Americans With Disabilities Act

The Americans with Disabilities Act (ADA) was modeled after the Vocational Rehabilitation Act of 1973 and the Rehabilitation Act of 1974. People with either mental or physical disabilities or limitations, or who are regarded as having such impairments, sometimes suffer from employment discrimination in that they are not considered for jobs that they are qualified for and are capable of doing. The ADA protects qualified individuals from unlawful discrimination in the workplace, including access to training and career development.

Defense Against Charges of Training Discrimination

It is not difficult to defend yourself against a charge of discrimination if you can show that your training programs are designed and delivered without bias. The following guidelines, from the Society for Human Resource Management (SHRM), apply to all of the employment laws discussed so far:

- Register affirmative action training and apprenticeship programs with the U.S. Department of Labor.
- Keep records of all employees who apply for enrollment in training programs and the details of how they were selected.
- Document all management decisions and actions that relate to the administration of training policies.
- Monitor each trainee's progress, provide evaluations, and ensure that counseling is available.
- Continue to evaluate results even after training is completed.

Labor Relations Statutes

Union activity between the 1930s and the mid-1950s provided the impetus for the development and passage of two acts that affect training and development: The National Labor Relations Act of 1935 (NLRA) and the Labor-Management Relations Act of 1947. The NLRA, also referred to as the Wagner Act, prohibits discrimination against union members with respect to terms and conditions of employment, including apprenticeships and training programs. The National Labor Relations Board considers training to be a condition of employment and a mandatory subject for collective bargaining. The Labor-Management Relations Act, also known as the Taft-Hartley Act, prevents unions from discriminating for any reason except for payment of dues and assessments. The act also permits noncoercive employer free speech; this may affect trainers. For example, if your company president supports a particular political party, it could be assumed that you support that party. In training, you should use no examples, case studies, or role plays that infringe upon a person's personal philosophy or belief system.

Copyright Statutes

Trainers try to use the very latest materials during training events. We must set an example that does not encourage others to use any material that requires prior permission for use.

The design and development of training programs likely requires the use or incorporation of various sources of information. It is important to pay attention to copyright requirements. Copyright, as defined by SHRM guidelines, is "...the exclusive right or privilege of the author or proprietor to print or otherwise multiply, distribute, and vend copies of his/her literary, artistic, or intellectual productions when secured by compliance with the copyright statute." This statute also gives the author the right to prepare derivative works.

The Copyright Act of 1976 stipulates that copyright begins with the creation of the work in a fixed form from which it can be perceived or communicated.

The exclusive rights of the author or proprietor are limited by the "fair use" of copyrighted works in certain circumstances. Whether a use is "fair" depends upon several factors, including:

- purpose
- nature
- amount
- effect on potential market value.

Fair use standards may apply to training materials. As a trainer, you can make a single copy of copyrighted materials for your own use. Check with the copyright holder before you make multiple copies of copyrighted materials. As SHRM points out, "if a trainer violates copyright statutes, the penalties can be severe and may include injunction, actual damages, defendant's lot profits, statutory damages, and attorney's fees."

For anonymous works and works made for hire (such as those prepared by trainers or other employees at the request of employers), the period of protection lasts for 75 years from the first year of publication or 100 years from the year of creation, whichever expires first. Employers, rather than employee who did the writing, are considered authors of the work and the owners of the copyright. SHRM points out that registration of the copyright with the Copyright Office of the Library of Congress is not a condition of copyright protection; the law does, however, provide inducement to register work.

A work that has fallen into the public domain is available for use without permission from the copyright owner or payment to that person. A work is considered public domain if it meets one of the following characteristics:

- It was published prior to January 1, 1978, without notice of copyright.
- The period of copyright protection has expired.

- It was produced for the U.S. government by its officers or employees as part of their official duties.

Until recently, copyrights had very little to do with the daily work of trainers. Intellectual property was easy to protect. However, with the advent of the Internet, it is easy for any computer user to copy, distribute, or publish virtually anything on the Internet. This technology threatens to make copyright and intellectual property safeguards obsolete. Copyright law blurs when it comes into contact with the Internet. However, messages or articles posted on a Usenet newsgroup or e-mail are automatically copyrighted by the authors.

BUDGETS

Figuring Training Costs

The goal of training and professional development in most organizations is to make a positive, cost-effective impact on the organization. Yet, the training department often appears as a departmental cost or organizational expense. Training provides significant return-on-investment and can be viewed as such rather than as a line-item expense in a budget.

Using traditional cost-accounting principles, you can show a return when you cost out your individual training programs. To do this, you must calculate the total cost of training. Next, indicate the savings or benefit to the organization. Finally, calculate the cost of training per employee. Here's the basic formula:

$$\frac{\text{Total cost of training}}{\text{Number of people trained}} = \text{cost per trainee}$$

The information needed to justify the cost of training depends on a number of factors. Table 5 shows the categories of potential costs and benefits. Actual costs will vary depending on the training site and whether programs have been custom-designed, purchased off-the-shelf, or developed in-house.

Considering Costs

You should include both direct and indirect costs in your overall training budget. Direct costs include regular operating costs, such as wages

Table 5. Potential training costs.	
POTENTIAL TRAINING COSTS	**POTENTIAL SAVINGS AND BENEFITS**

• Trainer's salary
• Trainee's salary or wage
• Materials and supplies for training
• Consultant's or contractor services
• Living expenses for trainer and trainees
• Cost of facilities
• Transportation
• Equipment
• Lost production (opportunity cost)
• Development costs:
  — Consultant's fees and expenses
  — Hours spent by staff professionals,
    clerical help, and line managers
• Support costs:
  — Postage
  — Data maintenance
• Equipment costs (may prorate):
  — Audiovisual
  — Computer
	• Reduction in errors
	• Increase in production
	• Reduction in turnover
	• Less supervision necessary
	• Ability to advance
	• Ability to perform wider range of jobs
	• Attitude change
	• Employee and organization alignment
	• Facilitation of organizational change
	• Improved customer satisfaction
	• Increase in organizational competencies

Source: Reprinted with permission of Society for Human Resource Management Certification Program, 1997.

or salaries of participants and trainers as well as costs for travel, lodging, supplies, and materials that relate to a particular program. Indirect costs include secretarial and clerical help, use of telephone and audiovisual equipment as well as costs associated with lower productivity when a worker is attending a training course.

When you prepare a budget proposal, include estimated savings or increased profits that might result from implementing the training. Include supplemental details for each program such as the following: program length, space requirements, number of trainees per session, materials, equipment, instructors (both internal and external), and an estimate of the development and administrative costs.

Most trainers look at cost figures to measure the impact of training success. Cost figures are taken directly from the budget and can be found in three general categories:

- Costs: expense per unit of training delivered
- Change: gain in skill or knowledge by the learner
- Impact: results or outcomes from the learner's use of new skills or knowledge.

No simple calculation can account for all possible training costs and benefits. However, the easiest calculation involves adding up all expenses (both direct and indirect) and dividing by the total number of people trained, as the following equation shows (SHRM, 1997).

$$\frac{\text{Cost of training}}{\text{Cost of unwanted behavior} \times \text{Probability of occurrence}} = \text{ROI}$$

Review the following example:

$$\text{ROI} = \frac{\$10{,}000 \text{ cost of training}}{\$190{,}000 \text{ cost of behavior} \times 10\% \text{ probability of occurrence}} = 53\%$$

This calculation indicates the cost of "targeted" training was $10,000. The cost of unwanted behavior to the organization was estimated to be $190,000. Once the "targeted" training program was delivered, the unwanted behavior would have a recurrence of only 10 percent of the time. The "targeted" training would immediately save the organization 53 percent of the projected $190,000 that would be lost if the unwanted behavior persisted.

Increasingly, trainers are being asked to demonstrate a return on training investment. Organizations are not willing to approve or continue to fund training and professional development programs unless they are aligned with the strategic and tactical plan and can be cost justified. Providing actual savings and showing a return on training investment can provide the tangible example that justifies the training budget. The key to your success is to design and deliver training interventions that are appropriate for all employees so that the skills and knowledge incorporated in the interventions contribute to corporate knowledge and competitive edge.

SUMMARY AND HIGHLIGHTS

Development is the process of creating, testing, and producing usable instructional materials. During the development process, choose instructional strategies that fit the needs of the perspective learners and that are appropriate to the content to be delivered.

Use the course module design template (table 2) to plan, organize, and develop the topic content, learner and trainer activities, and required peripherals; and use the support requirements list (table 1) for making decisions about the learning activities to ensure successful training transfer.

Review the instructional strategies and their meaning before you start to construct your training program and develop the learning activities. You use an instructional strategy or peripheral to amplify the learning incident. These strategies should not be integrated into the training design just to provide an activity period, but they should contribute and guide the learning process to achieve an outcome.

Remember to develop a training design report after you've conducted an initial investigation of the problem and situation and found that the identified problem could be resolved with training. The design report is a summary of the work you've completed to date. The report serves three purposes: It is a summary of the results of the analysis and design work completed thus far, a communication tool for key management to ensure that training meets their expectations, and a method for the training manager or director to use to supervise the various stages of the design and development of this project.

Calculate the training costs correctly. Use traditional cost accounting principles designed to determine the total cost of training. Once this is done and you've established a measurement mechanism within the training program to measure behavior change, you can then calculate the return-on-investment (ROI).

Note

The Society for Human Resource Management has done extensive research in this area. If you require additional definition or interpretation of the legal and regulatory factors that impact training intervention and budgeting, contact SHRM, 1800 Duke St., Alexandria, VA 22314; 703.548.3440; www.shrm.org.

6

Implementation

INTRODUCTION

Implementation, or delivery, is the link between design and development and the training need or opportunity. It involves providing the necessary training for instructors and conducting the actual training. All of the delivery procedures were established during the design stage. Implementation itself carries out the goals and objectives of the program, and it provides the data for assessing program effectiveness. This stage works together with evaluation, which is described in chapter 7, and some of the steps outlined in the next chapter must be carried out before a training program can be successfully implemented.

In the simplest terms, implementation is the delivery of training. It is holding a conversation with your audience. A successful conversation requires audience interest, well-organized topics, and a method to check for understanding. This chapter provides tools for preparing and presenting your training session. The tools will become part of the skills portfolio that you bring to any conversation.

People often become frightened when they prepare to deliver training or a speech or even when they prepare to audition for a community theater's annual production. Rather than think in terms of fear, think in terms of opportunity. Delivery is an opportunity to show your "stuff." As you proceed through this chapter, think opportunity. The following suggestions will help you develop effective training presentations

- Do your homework.
- Know your audience.
- Organize your content.
- Rely on facts, not opinions.
- Use examples.
- Establish high standards.
- Speak at the audience's level.
- Treat all trainees as your equals.
- Answer all questions (admit not knowing an answer).
- Think positively.
- Exude enthusiasm.
- Smile.

Every member of your audience will take away a piece of you, regardless the type of training you're doing. More than business justification, the implementation of training—delivery—is what people will remember. This chapter provides proven methods for ensuring you are remembered as an effective and enthusiastic trainer. The chapter is divided in two parts: preparation and presentation.

PREPARATION

Preparation is your best defense against seemingly unmanageable fear. With careful preparation, you can reduce and control your nervousness. Plan the preparation, know your audience and the physical setting, and select appropriate materials and a comfortable format.

Step One: Plan the Presentation

The most essential and the most time-consuming step is the first one, when you plan your presentation. Planning requires establishing the topic and subtopic areas, understanding the audience's needs, sequencing the topics for logical and easy learning, and building these into the presentation.

First, you must determine the purpose. Trainers often confuse purpose with objectives so it is important to understand the difference. The purpose is a single, broadly stated goal, the one result you want your delivery to achieve. (See chapter 4, "Design," for the explanation of objectives as they relate to delivery of a training session.)

Next, you must focus on a single purpose. Think of your purpose first in terms of the audience, the trainees. Remember that your purpose is to effect a change in them. You want them to think or behave differently or to have acquired new knowledge as a result of your presentation. You will determine the purpose on the basis of your needs assessment.

The following are examples of training purposes:

- Teach newly promoted managers how to be effective in their new roles.

- Show technicians how to service the organization's computers.

- Illustrate how sales staff can improve customer relations.

- Demonstrate computerized reservation systems to new travel agents.

Step Two: Know the Audience and the Venue

As part of the preparation of your delivery, you must have information about two essential elements: the audience and the physical setting.

Know Your Audience

Every audience, even a training group, has a single definite personality, regardless of the many personalities and characteristics of individual members. Listed below are many questions you can ask to learn about your audience. Often called audience analysis, this step is critical to the preparation of a successful delivery.

- Your audience's jobs:
    — What are their job titles and functions?
    — Are they managers, teachers, or physicians?
    — Are they parents, young adults, men, women, or older adults?

- Their knowledge of this topic:
    — What do they know?
    — Have they heard similar presentations?
    — Is this topic new to them?
    — What is important to learn?

— What do they need to know?

— Are they coming for general knowledge or for specific skills?

— If they are coming to learn specific skills, what kind of skills (for example, job, personal, career, coping)?

— What is not important to learn?

— What do they not need to know?

— How much do they already know about the subject?

— What will they consider superfluous or boring?

• Consider their sensitivities:

— What should you risk talking about?

— What kinds of backgrounds do they have?

— Is there anything in your background that you could share?

— What topics might insult their beliefs or their intelligence?

— What are their attitudes?

— How can you build credibility?

• External issues:

— What time of day is the training?

— What kind of atmosphere exists?

— Will attendees be in a rush to leave at the end?

— Will attendees be drifting in and out during the presentation?

— Are they eager to learn or are they skeptical about training?

— What are they interested in learning?

— Who is paying for them to attend?

As you proceed through the steps of preparing your delivery, always keep your audience in mind. Neglecting your audience could sabotage the training presentation.

You will need to determine the audience's level of knowledge about your topic. Levels will vary greatly. Some members of the audience may know more than you do about particular points, whereas others may not know enough to follow your delivery.

An audience's knowledge falls into the following five categories:

• no knowledge

• below average knowledge

• average knowledge

- above average knowledge

- expert.

Armed with this information, you can select an effective strategy. You have two basic choices:

- For an informal or general presentation, you can aim at the average.

- For specific skill training, you should ask, "In which of the five categories does the discerning mind sit?" If you miss by more than one category, you will not accomplish your training objectives.

If you are unsure about the audience's level of knowledge, be careful.

- Do not underestimate the audience's intelligence.

- Do not overestimate the audience's knowledge and experience.

- Remember, part of knowing your audience is understanding that the audience members want you to succeed.

Know the Physical Setting

Knowing the configuration of the room in which you will be delivering the training is important because you can use the specifics to enhance the presentation. The size and shape of the room, the seating arrangement, and your location relative to that of the audience are critical factors to consider in the preparation phase.

Seating is usually arranged according to one of the following styles:

- U-shaped. A U-shaped arrangement is ideal for groups of 15 to 30 people. Everyone can see and interact with everyone else, while attention is focused on you, the speaker.

- Small group. This arrangement is best when your audience will spend time working or discussing issues in small groups. A small group arrangement is good for technical presentations, where the goal is to instruct. Similar to the U-shaped arrangement, the small group style enables you to walk among your audience. This arrangement also is good for all types of visual aids.

- Conference table. This arrangement works for formal and informal meetings of up to 12 people. A conference table style is particularly effective for using flipcharts, as described later.

- Theater. This arrangement permits the greatest number of seats in the smallest amount of space. Theater style is good and often necessary for groups of more than 50, especially if the room size is limited. You should be aware that theater style limits discussion and requires a more formal presentation. You will need to ensure that all members of the audience can see you and your visual aids.

Similar to the series of questions you might ask to get to know your audience, you might ask some of the following questions to get to know the physical setting:

- Is the room properly lighted? You must be able to see the audience and the audience must be able to see you. Enthusiasm, inspiration, or motivation is almost impossible to communicate in a poorly lit room.
- Does the room have cool, fresh air? A room that is too warm and has still air will put your audience to sleep, especially after a meal.
- Is the speaking area neat, and does it look professional? The place from which you make your delivery is your personal space, and your audience will judge you by its appearance.

Step Three: Select Materials and Format

Once you know your audience and the physical surroundings in which the training will take place, you are in a better position to select the most appropriate materials and format to use in your presentation. In making selections for all training presentations, you must consider the trainees and the content.

Trainees

When designing the format of your presentation, the most important consideration is the trainees. The way to ensure that trainees respond to your program is to address the following four critical issues as you design your format:

- Content base: One of the principles of adult learning theory is that adults learn nothing new. Adults merely sort and fit the concepts presented in the training into their existing knowledge base.

- Motivation: You do not have the power to motivate anyone to learn. However, you can create environments and opportunities for people to learn by making the training immediately applicable on the job or by ensuring that the training contributes to the trainees' personal and professional growth, or by doing both.

- Responsibility: As the trainer, it is your job to help trainees share the responsibility for what it is they are about to learn.

- Types of learning skills: In general, people learn by seeing, listening, or doing. Regardless of the type of learning preference or strategy your trainees possess, all of them learn best when there is a structured lesson plan.

Content

Content is the information, knowledge, or skills you intend to impart. When deciding how to develop the content, first decide whether the presentation should focus on the trainer (known as a trainer-centered presentation) or on those being trained (trainee centered). In making this decision, consider the learning outcome, the simplicity or complexity of the content, your skill level as a trainer, and the trainees' level of learning.

Table 1 displays formats for training programs, according to the focus of the presentation. The left column lists trainer-centered formats in which the trainer is responsible for presentations of theory or skills or is the lecturer. In the right column, there is a list of trainee-centered programs.

Table 1. Training formats to match presentations.

TRAINER CENTERED	IN BETWEEN	TRAINEE CENTERED
Theory	Case study	Contract learning
Skills	Role play	Computer based
Lecture	Simulation	Programmed instruction

Contract learning, computer based, and programmed instruction provide the opportunity for learners to assert their control over the content that they are to master. These formats let them decide the parameters for learning the content at a time, place, and learning pace.

The middle column, in between, lists learning formats that provide learning experiences that represent a partnership in which learners and the trainer take equal roles and responsibilities in the learning process.

How do you collect content? One easy way to begin is by jotting down ideas as soon as you know you are going to give a training presentation. To generate more ideas, use brainstorming techniques in which you write down anything that comes to mind regardless of its practicality. Remember that you are simply collecting content. As you select content, you do not need to use every note; you merely need to use the best of the ridiculous or impossible ideas you have noted.

Trust yourself to know what content is best. The simple act of trusting yourself allows you to get out of your own way as you gather ideas by not judging those ideas as you jot them down. You are the authority on your subject even if others don't recognize you as such. By virtue of your own experience, you are qualified to speak with authority about experiences and events in your personal and professional life. Weave these experiences and events into your delivery to make points, expand on issues, or use as examples. In doing so, you will put yourself and your audience at ease. In fact, as you collect and select ideas, remember that you are merely having a conversation with your equals, which is what training is.

If after reviewing your notes, you believe your idea generation is a bit weaker than you would like, you can gather additional information through literature searches, personal observations, experiments, surveys, and interviews. Unless your subject is scholarly or extremely technical, you can probably find all the written material you need in books, magazines, and technical manuals.

PRESENTATION

Step Four: Organize the Presentation

Tips abound for the best way to organize the materials you have collected and selected. One of the easiest ways to get started putting all the materials together is to write the purpose of the training (see "Step One: Plan the Presentation" at the beginning of this chapter) in large letters on paper and tape it on the wall in front of you. Then, create a mental picture of the audience you have identified clearly. Remember that most training presentations have one of two basic purposes: to present information or develop a skill. Correspondingly, there are two types of training presentations: information oriented (theory) or skill related.

The information-oriented presentation, or theory session, stresses ideas, whereas the skill-related presentation, or skill session, stresses mastery of a particular skill. Often the training topic will dictate which model to apply. At times, however, the training topic will be more ambiguous so that as the trainer, you may consider applying either or both models.

Assume that you were asked to train employees on how to fill out a newly required form. By reviewing the training presentation's objectives (see chapter 3, "Analysis") you may obtain a clearer understanding of which model to use.

Do the trainees only need to learn how to complete the form? Or must the trainees also understand the reason that the new form is being required and how that new form relates to work processes or communication? If the objective is to fill out the form and also to understand the new form's role in work processes, then combine a theory session, in which you explain the role of the form, with a skill session, in which you show how to complete the form.

Theory Session Model

Assume you are beginning with a theory session because trainers often precede a skill session with a theory session during which they present background information about the skill. The theory session model, as figure 1 shows, usually consists of three segments: introduction, body, and closure. First divide your presentation into these segments, each of which may be relatively independent of one another or may build sequentially upon the other. Each segment needs its own objective.

The introduction is an essential step in setting the tone and direction or intent of the training. Although this is the first part, prepare it last. Remember, you must accomplish the following in your introduction, although you will not have covered some of these points until you have designed and developed the content and selected the appropriate training strategies.

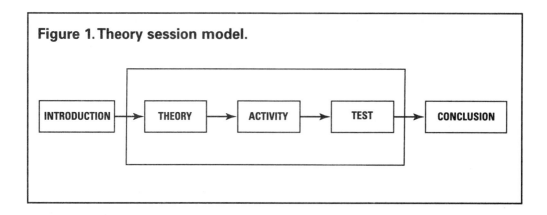

Figure 1. Theory session model.

INTRODUCTION → THEORY → ACTIVITY → TEST → CONCLUSION

- Gain trainees' interest.
- Check trainees' current knowledge.
- Orient trainees.
- Preview your material.
- Motivate trainees.

You need backup information to support each phase in the body of your presentation: the theory, activity, and test. In the body, you must present your major points in logical order.

The conclusion, which briefly reviews the topic and major points, serves three functions:

- It links material together.
- It clarifies issues.
- It ends the presentation.

Time and schedule are important considerations when organizing the presentation. Training programs often have tight schedules, and you must allocate a specific amount of time for presenting a specific amount of information. You must plan to maximize learning per unit of time.

Assume 60 minutes has been allocated for your theory session presentation. As you know from the last chapter, you typically have 55 minutes in each hour for your presentation. The introduction and conclusion each take 5 percent of the time, which would be approximately two and a half minutes each.

Divide the remaining 50 minutes not necessarily equally among the body segments.

Usually you will spend less time on the theory segment than on the activity and test segments. In the 55-minute presentation, allocate 10 minutes to the theory segment and 20 minutes each to the activity and test segments.

When using the theory session model, you may need to fabricate an activity that facilitates your ability to observe if the trainees will have attained the training objective.

Skill Session Model

As figure 2 shows, the skill session also has three components. Unlike the body in the theory session, in the skill session the body includes practice. The introduction in the skill session has three main parts:

- Gain trainees' interest.
- Check trainees' current knowledge.
- Orient trainees.

The body contains three actions:

- Show.
- Show and tell.
- Provide trainees practice opportunities.

The conclusion serves three functions:

- It links material together.
- It clarifies issues.
- It ends the presentation.

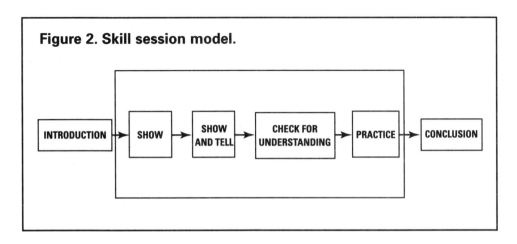

Figure 2. Skill session model.

INTRODUCTION → SHOW → SHOW AND TELL → CHECK FOR UNDERSTANDING → PRACTICE → CONCLUSION

Unlike the theory session model in which you may have to create an activity in which to observe whether trainees have attained the training objective, in the skill session model you readily observe trainees performing the task and applying the content of the session directly. The skill session is all about physical activity (the behavioral component of the objective).

In organizing the skill session, you will break the task down into a series of closely linked steps of physical activity. By having trainees repeatedly practice the steps, you allow them the chance to perform the task more proficiently (measured in terms of time taken and quality of output).

To help you know that you have explained the task successfully, trainees should be able to perform the specified task in less than 10 percent of the total length of the session. Again, using the 55-minute session as an example, trainees have time to learn a five-and-a-half-minute task.

Plan the Introduction

You have probably often heard that you get only one chance to make a first impression. This adage holds for your presentation. During your first few sentences, you win or lose your audience. The purpose of your introduction is to open up the trainees' minds so they will be receptive to your delivery and to get the trainees involved immediately in your presentation. In the introduction, tell the audience what the presentation is about and relate the introduction to your overall purpose for giving the presentation. There are several methods you can use in the introduction:

- Ask a question.
- Make a dramatic statement.
- Appeal to a special interest of your audience.
- Use visual aids.
- Tell a story, anecdote, or personal experience.
- Use a quotation.

Plan the Body

As you organize the presentation, keep in mind that the body is the development of a statement. A statement can do a variety of things, including the following:

- Express an idea.
- Make a judgment.
- Offer an opinion.
- Provide a fact.
- Present a matter of inquiry.

You can develop any of these statements through illustration, interpretation, or reinforcement. You can use the following materials to support your development of each statement:

- *Fact:* Statistic, data, something that can be proved, such as a typical circumstance or characteristic case to make the statement clear, vivid, and credible.
- *Comparison and contrast:* A likeness or difference that associates the new with the familiar.
- *Testimony:* The say-so of someone other than you, preferably a well-known authority.
- *Quotation:* Type of testimony that is short and to the point. (Note: A testimony is a firsthand verification of a fact; a quotation is a passage in someone's exact words.)
- *Digression:* Built-in element that allows you to act as if you were departing from your script to tell a secret or to relate something that just popped into your head.
- *Demonstration:* You show while the audience watches you perform the action.
- *Visual aid:* Laptop computer projected on a screen, 35-mm slides, wall charts or learning maps, 3-D models or drawings add some pizzazz and interest to your presentation, make your points vivid, and help your audience remember the material.

Remember as you develop the body that each major point is a minipresentation with its own introduction, body, and conclusion.

Plan the Conclusion

Briefly review your topic and the major points, and provide a summary that states the most important point of the presentation. Here is a list of techniques that assist in summarizing the learning content. You may do one or more of these steps in sequence or simultaneously. You make you choice by considering the topic, the learners' abilities and accomplishments, and the learners' preferences:

- Appeal for action by stating what you want the trainees to do.
- State your conclusion.
- Relate the conclusion to the introduction.
- Ask a question.
- Use a dynamic quotation.
- Stress the relationship of your topic to the trainees' interests.
- Pay your audience a compliment.

If you remember only one thing about the conclusion, remember that when you close, close. End your presentation. Make the ending memorable.

Plan the Method of Delivery

When thinking about how you will deliver your presentation, remember, again, that you are holding a conversation with your audience. Although at first you might think it would be easier, or at least less frightening, to read or memorize your presentation, if you do, you will not really be engaged in conversation. Imagine the times you have interrupted a direct telephone marketer to ask a question, and the person on the other end does not know what to do. Imagine yourself as that person if you were to deliver your presentation by reading or memorizing it.

Read or memorized presentations often sound artificial, and they create unwanted distance between the presenter and the audience. Because you want to effect a change in behavior, you do not want to run the risk of losing your audience. It can be helpful to memorize certain sections of your presentation, for example, the introduction and the conclusion, as will be explained later. A read or memorized presentation leaves little room for spontaneity or for responding to your audience. In fact, by reading or delivering a memorized presentation, you may be insulting your audience. If that weren't enough to discourage you from reading or memorizing, then think of this: You need to practice long and hard to read well, much longer than practicing presenting material as a conversation.

If you are most comfortable reading a presentation, include some of the following extra aids in your script:

- colored pens
- slash marks to represent places to pause
- underlined statements for emphasis
- enlarged punctuation marks for exclamation or questions.

Also, enclose passages that you can memorize in boxes so that you can look at your audience when you delivery them.

Think of memorization as another form of reading—reading from within. Rather than looking at your notes, you are searching your brain for the information you prepared. Memorization suffers from most of the same disadvantages as reading, especially the inability to maintain eye contact with the trainees.

Extemporaneous delivery is best and has some of the following advantages:

- It adapts to a variety of circumstances.
- It encourages audience involvement and interaction.
- It projects spontaneity and enthusiasm regardless of how often you deliver the same presentation.
- It injects interest and enthusiasm.

For the extemporaneous delivery method, you must plan and thoroughly rehearse your presentation and write the presentation as part of your preparation. For an extemporaneous delivery, you do not bring your script, but you do bring notes to serve as reminders of the introduction and conclusion, key statistics, and catch words and phrases that you will use as main points.

Step Five: Create the Presentation

This is it. Now you must create the presentation you will deliver. Creating a presentation is actually less threatening than writing essays or business reports because no one will review your grammar, punctuation, or spelling. Again, remember that you are writing a conversation. You are creating a lasting impression designed to effect a change in behavior. You are leaving your listeners with memories.

As you write your presentation, be yourself and write in a conversational style as if you were writing a friend a letter. Although you will have everything you need, by the time you are ready to sit down to create the presentation, make sure you give yourself more than one day to create it. The longer the training session, the more time you will need to allow for preparing the delivery of the session.

Good presentations are clear, concise, and to the point and although they are conversations, the language is more formal than that of ordinary casual conversations. As described earlier, you must choose your words carefully (see chapter 4, table 1, "Fuzzy Words").

Words

Words can be simple and produce an image of the object named. Use words that are as specific as possible to help your audience see, hear, feel, smell, or taste what you mean. Words also can be complex and have more than one meaning. Sometimes words are misleading, and often they are only close approximations of true meanings.

The following tips may help you choose your words:

- Use familiar words. In general, familiar words are easier to understand than fancy words. Familiar words tend to be shorter, more concrete, and more vivid.

- Be careful with technical terms and business jargon. The preparation you did during the second step, "Know the Audience and the Venue," will help you limit your words to your audience's level. Even if you believe your audience will understand technical words, do not use them (it is best not to assume anything). Use technical terms and business jargon only when you know every person in the audience will understand the words.

- Use concrete and specific words. You can help yourself to use concrete and specific words if you use examples or vignettes that a member of the audience provided you during the presentation rather than the "canned" examples that you use all the time. To do this, you will have to listen carefully and integrate the content and the process of the training that you are facilitating. At times you will want to use abstract concepts, such as justice, good, or profit, rather than specific words. Be sure to clarify the meaning by giving examples or illustrations. Be specific whenever you can. Rather than referring vaguely to a large city in southern California, for example, say San Diego if you mean San Diego or Los Angeles if you mean Los Angeles.

- Use action words. Use the best action words you can to describe the training. Search, if you must, for action words that suggest movement or convey what they mean either by how they sound or by their imagery. Consider solid words such as *slash* rather than *cut, shred* rather than *crumble,* and *shout* rather than *say.*

- Use figures of speech such as similes and metaphors. A simile is a comparison of two things that, in general, are not considered part of the same universe. Similes are introduced by the word *as* or *like,* as in *cheeks like an apple* and *hair like corn silk.* A metaphor is an implied comparison.

Visual Aids

As you write your presentation, think of how you can use visual aids and incorporate them. Visual materials have several benefits. They do the following:

- arouse interest
- encourage participation
- prevent misunderstanding
- persuade
- focus attention
- save time
- reinforce ideas
- add humor
- enhance credibility
- explain the inaccessible.

Visual materials supplement your presentation. Do not use visual materials as a script, but rather as a checklist of key ideas you will explain, expand upon, and emphasize.

The following are types of visual aids:

- *Charts:* Charts can be configured as words, as an organizational structure, as a pie, or as a series of sheets of paper.
  — Word charts are lists and tables that you can prepare quickly. When creating word charts, use the seven-seven rule: limit lines of type to seven; limit words per line to seven.

— Organization charts are useful to explain processes and operations.
— Pie charts show percentage distribution, with the circle or pie representing the whole and the segments, the parts. When using pie charts, make sure everyone in the audience can see the smallest part. Consider putting in different colors the segment or segments you want to emphasize.
— Flipcharts are large, blank sheets of paper, bound at the top. The original flipcharts were made from the large sheets of newsprint paper that companies used to print newspapers. Now, another brand of flipchart is available that has a sticky portion at the top back of each flip page to enable it to adhere to a surface. No more looking for tape to hang those charts on the wall!

Most facilities in which you will be presenting your training have flipcharts and markers available on-site. If you need to improve your handwriting on flipcharts, or even on white boards, practice. Try holding the markers at different angles until you are satisfied that you see some improvement. For years, I used the wrong angle of the marker. Because I was left-handed, I thought my difficulty with writing was fate until one day someone asked me to draw a line on the flipchart, and I used the fat side of the marker. What a surprise! I had a great looking line. Then I started to write better using the appropriate angle of the marker. Try it. Experiment with pens and markers. Find the ones that work best for you.

Flipcharts lose their effectiveness when used for groups of more than 40 people. When using flipcharts, be sure to direct your attention to the audience, not the flipcharts.

- *Cutaways:* Cutaways are a technique for showing aspects of the interior of an object in such a way as to clarify the spatial relationships.
- *Maps:* Maps should include only the specific features of land or sea that serve the purpose of the presentation. Eliminate elements that do not enhance your purpose.
- *Graphs:* Several types of graphs are used commonly:
  — line graphs, which show how related sets of facts change according to a common measure of reference, usually time

— profile graphs, which present the same sort of information using shadowing or coloring

— bar graphs, which compare two facts, but do not show how they change over time.

- *Projected visual aids:* Computer-generated slides projected from laptop computers are fast becoming the most commonly used visual aid. Other types of projected visual aids are 35-mm slides and overhead transparencies. Projected visual aids are useful for large groups because everyone in the audience can see them. They also give trainers control over the image because they can turn the projector off. Projected visual aids can easily lend themselves to humor and help generate a sense of community among trainees who do not know one another. Following are some rules to keep in mind when using projected visual aids:

— Illustrate one idea only per slide.

— Use only 15 words per slide.

— Make sure the letters are legible.

— Keep the content simple.

— Use color whenever possible.

— Use several consecutive slides to explain complex information.

Most facilities have overhead projectors on hand. Consider using overhead projectors when you want to show the following types of items:

— *transparencies:* Transparencies are easy to photocopy and distribute to the audience after the presentation.

— *text and photos from other sources:* Your daily newspaper often contains the very item that will enhance your presentation. Also check books or magazines.

— *cartoons:* Use cartoons carefully to make sure they do not offend any member of the audience. You can turn an ordinary photograph into a cartoon by adding an incongruous caption.

- *Models, mockups, and props.* These types of visual aids have high-impact value, but often can be expensive and time-consuming to prepare. The biggest advantage of using models, mockups, and props is that they add realism to your presentation because of their three dimensions.

For the most effective use of any visual aid, keep in mind the following points:

- *Size and visibility:* The visual aid must be large enough so everyone in the audience can see it clearly and read it easily. Audiences find visual aids that they cannot see annoying and distracting. Instead of paying attention to what the visual aid is communicating, audience members are desperately contorting themselves so as to see the image. To make your visual aids large enough so everyone can see them, you need to know the physical setting in which the training will take place (refer to step two). If you can, experiment with the visual aids in the actual room in which you will be delivering your presentation.
- *Details:* Details that are not essential to your point can detract from your presentation. Unless decoration is the point you are trying to make, do not be decorative.
- *Precision:* Make sure your visual aids are neat and precise. Sloppy or careless visual aids reflect poorly on you as a trainer.
- *Focus:* Remember that your eyes are on the audience, not on the visual aids. The trainees' eyes must be on the visual aids.
- *Introduction:* Every visual aid needs to be put into context. First state what the visual aid is intended to show and then point out its main features.
- *Planning:* Incorporate your visual aids into your script and rehearse them exactly as you plan to present them. Do not show a visual aid until you are ready to talk about it, and as soon as you are finished talking about it, remove it from sight.

Perhaps the most important reason to use visual materials is that people learn more through sight than through any other sense. Visual material helps people retain what they learn. As table 2 shows, people retain information longer in presentations that both show and tell. Trainees are likely to remember much more, much longer if you show as well as tell your presentation.

You can help your audience retain what you present by adhering to the KISS and KILL principles:

Table 2. Retention and presentation method.

	PERCENTAGE OF INFORMATION RETAINED	
Presentation method	After 3 hours	After 3 days
Tell only	70	10
Show only	72	20
Show and tell	85	65

- KISS: Keep It Simple and Succinct
- KILL: Keep It Legible and Large

Editing Tips

After you have completed preparing the presentation, put it away for at least a day or two. Then come back to the presentation and read it aloud critically. You will be amazed at what reading aloud uncovers. As you read it aloud, you have time to revise the language and sentence structure as more fitting words and phrases come to mind or as you trip over clumsy and unclear sentences.

Learn to be your own harshest critic, which for some of us is not difficult. Some of us have long been our own harshest critics and make unreasonable demands on ourselves. By editing your presentation before anyone else has seen it, you can save yourself from an audience of editors and critics, some of whom love nothing more than finding glitches in an expert's presentation.

As you edit, ask yourself the following questions:

- Does the material fit the purpose?
- Does the organization follow the objectives?
- Are the main points properly balanced in terms of presentation time and amount of coverage?
- Are any points unnecessarily duplicated?
- Is the presentation written in a conversational style?

- Does sentence length vary?
- Do any sentences seem too long?
- Have you included enough illustrations, examples, comparisons, statistics, and quotes?
- Will you be able to acknowledge contradictory views and refute them?
- Are there enough benefits to persuade?

Presentation Notes

Even though you have prepared your presentation in every respect, know your audience and the physical setup, and organized your material, you still must prepare for something to go wrong. Easy-to-follow notes can help you overcome most of the annoying mishaps you are likely to encounter. You must be able to see your notes in bright or dim lights and when you change your position to accommodate visual aids. The following tips can help you prepare your presentation notes:

- Use a large typeface.
- Double or triple space between lines and double that space between paragraphs.
- Use hanging indents for paragraphs so the first line will be easy to spot.
- Keep a complete sentence on one page and whenever possible keep an entire paragraph on one page.
- Put six periods at the end of sentences, so you do not run them together accidentally.
- Type words the way you will say them (for example, one-and-a-half million dollars not $1,500,000).
- Use only one side of the sheet of paper and do not fasten the sheets in any way.
- Number the sheets of paper.
- Mark where visual aids occur exactly by putting a key word or a sketch in the margin.

Rehearsals

Half of the preparation for your presentation is rehearsal. As the presenter you are the playwright and the cast. By practicing in as many ways as possible, you will find that you are thoroughly prepared. Consider adhering to the following suggestions:

- Rehearse enough to learn your presentation and then go through the entire presentation each time you rehearse. If you make a mistake or omit an item, proceed as if you were actually delivering the presentation. This teaches you to deal more easily with mistakes.

- Reduce relying on your notes more and more as you rehearse. If you can make mental notes of the important points of your introduction and your conclusion, you will have an easier time maintaining continuous eye contact with the audience during these critical parts of the presentation.

- Practice with a tape recorder. Listen to your voice to hear if it sounds pleasant, lively, and interesting. Do your pace, inflection, and pitch vary, or do you sound monotonous? Does your voice trail off at the end of sentences?

- Videotape your rehearsal. Check gestures, eye contact, body movement, and how you interact with your visual aids; listen to your voice. Pay attention to repeated mannerisms that may be annoying, such as pushing hair out of your face or saying "you know."

- Rehearse in front of people. Pay attention to the rehearsal audience's comments and trust your own opinions. Rehearsing in front of people will help you feel more confident and prepared for your delivery.

- Practice ad-libbing. If you do not read your script, you will undoubtedly ad-lib. By practicing, you will feel more comfortable during the actual delivery.

- Dress for a dress rehearsal. Wear what you plan to wear during the delivery, which will help you discover how well your attire will react to movements and gestures. Dress comfortably and appropriately.

Your Personality

Use your personality, your nervousness, or your enthusiasm to your advantage.

You will discover some things about your personality each time you rehearse. When you think of delivery as an opportunity rather than a frightening prospect, you will have an easier time adopting the following tips:

- Pretend that you are brave.
- Focus your attention on the subject of the presentation and move your mind off yourself.
- Convert fear into positive nervousness by accepting rather than resisting fear.
- Enjoy yourself and think of your fears as opportunities.
- Avoid stimulants or depressants such as caffeine or alcohol.
- Do isometrics while waiting to give your introduction.
- Pay attention to your breathing to ensure you are breathing rhythmically.

This chapter began by mentioning people's fear of making presentations. Don't let your fear control your delivery. Remember that everything gets easier after you do it several times, especially if you use the tips provided.

Much of training is preparing to peak at the moment of performance. Athletes prepare physically and mentally for just such moments, and you can do the same. Your attitude more than your ability will win an audience. Employers often select a more enthusiastic candidate, rather than a more qualified one. You can ensure that you'll make a successful delivery by sharing your enthusiasm with your audience. Enthusiasm shows that you believe in yourself and in your subject.

Be careful not to fake enthusiasm. Your audience will sense immediately if you are not being genuine. By accepting and understanding that a warm and spontaneous delivery is better than a perfect one, you will guarantee being naturally enthusiastic. Yes, be dramatic, but appropriately so. Exaggeration is an important and necessary element of oral communication. Remember, most likely you will not have exciting scenery or backdrops for your presentation, so let your personality be some of the scenery.

Techniques for Success

If there is an opportunity before you begin your delivery, mingle with your audience projecting a friendly, confident attitude. If there is no such opportunity, see if you can rework the schedule ever so slightly so as to create the opportunity to gather with your audience first.

Once you are introduced as the presenter, walk briskly with purpose and confidence to the speaking position. Immediately connect with your audience, glancing at people with whom you have just mingled. Smile and limit your movements and gestures during the first few minutes of your presentation.

Begin speaking at a low pitch, yet loud enough so as to be heard. Stand about six to eight inches away from the microphone. Even if you are shaking in your shoes or your hands are trembling, keep going and do not pay attention to your feet or your hands. After a few minutes, you will relax and be on your way to a successful delivery.

In general, if you can begin by making a remark or two that directly pertains to your specific audience, you will be telling the audience members that you understand them. If possible, tell them something they did not think you would know about them as a group. As simple as it might sound, your audience will be interested in you if you show you are interested in them.

Be positive and confident and never apologize or make excuses for anything. For example, the full-service shop that you have relied on to turn your sketches into dynamic visual aids might not have come through as it usually does. Don't reveal this disappointment with your audience.

Delivery is the stage at which everything comes together. Through your knowledge, authority, concern, and confidence, which you communicate through your appearance, gestures, face, eyes, and voice and the content of your presentation, you will be as good as it gets when it comes to delivery.

Body Language

Who hasn't heard time and again that actions speak louder than words? It's true. People are always sending messages through their body, even when they're not speaking. Your body will communicate the following to your audience:

- your sincerity
- your enjoyment in making the presentation
- your belief in what you are communicating
- your interest in your audience and that you care about them
- your confidence in the situation and control of it.

Your goal is to use gestures purposefully, not randomly. To the extent possible, do the following:

- Control your gestures without being stiff.
- Be spontaneous without being contrived.
- Be dramatic without being theatrical.

Let your body speak naturally just as you would in a conversation. Erect and relaxed posture conveys poise and confidence. Graceful, fluid movements convey purpose and thought, and precise and spontaneous gestures convey life and meaning.

Facial Expression

Your audience will assume the emotions you project. If your face shows excitement, your audience will begin to feel excited. If you look dour or afraid, you audience will begin to reflect that.

As with body language, facial expressions must always be appropriate. And while smiling is almost always recommended to connect you to your audience, if you are talking about a tragedy or making a demand, smiling would be inappropriate.

Check your facial expressions for animation, friendliness, naturalness, and appropriateness.

Vocal Message

A strong pleasant voice is one of your greatest assets as a speaker. Breathing has a lot to do with the strength of your voice. You give yourself the best chance for success by standing up straight with your stomach tucked in so the diaphragm gets the support it needs to enable your lungs to fill deeply with air. Posture supplies the diaphragm the support it needs.

A good speaking voice is

- pleasant and conveys warmth
- natural and reflects your personality
- dynamic and gives an impression of strength without being loud
- expressive and reveals shades of meaning and emotion
- articulate and makes it easy to understand what you are saying.

Check for the following when delivering your presentation:

- *Volume:* Is your voice audible, appropriately strong, and variable for emphasis?
- *Pitch:* Is your voice low pitched and melodic, conveying color?
- *Pace:* Do you speak neither too fast nor too slow, without hesitations or jerks? Do you speak smoothly, fluently, and with deliberately varied speed?
- *Articulation:* Do you mumble, speak lazily, or mispronounce words?
- *Vocal quality:* Is your voice nasal, breathy, harsh, raspy, or lifeless?
- *Vocal variety:* Is your voice dull, strained, or lacking in emotion? Is your voice varied in pitch, volume, timing, and inflection, conveying emotion and vitality?

Eye Contact

Throughout your presentation, maintain eye contact with the entire audience. Avoid focusing on only a few people or on one side of the room. At all times your eye contact should be natural and smooth and should not follow a set pattern.

Eye contact is your most powerful body language. The simple act of looking a person squarely in the eye is more persuasive than a hundred words.

Look at one person and hold eye contact with that person until you get a response. Then move to another person. Keep doing this with people all around the room. If you did not have an opportunity to mingle with the audience before being introduced, then pick friendly faces as the first ones with whom to make eye contact. After you have warmed up and you sense the trainees are with you, focus on less friendly faces.

Step Six: Manage the Audience

Now that you have reached your defining moment in the delivery, you are ready to show your stuff. You have planned and organized your presentation and you have learned about your audience and about the physical setting in which you are about to reside temporarily. Here you are engaged in conversation with your trainee group, your equals, and you imagine that everything you have prepared is designed to generate responses. Regardless of the level of perfection you have achieved in your rehearsals, you are never really certain of what kind of reaction or response your delivery will generate. However, because of your rehearsals and your experience and because you are an authority, you will manage the audience successfully. You will adapt to your audience's responses. As members of the audience respond, be confident that you will adjust your delivery, both content and presentation style, accordingly.

But what if your worst fears are realized and your audience seems to be looking around the room and not at you, or worse, what if they seem to be falling asleep? If you recognize this kind of response, risk more not less. Make your delivery more dramatic. Identify a few sympathetic looking faces and play to them. Communicate an increased level of caring about your audience.

If you sense that there might be a problem, ask the audience members to share their concern or discuss the situation with you. It is best to clarify an issue or problem, not to ignore it. It's best for everyone concerned that you know what's going on: best for the learners to know that you know that they know and that you want to help understand and engage in problem solving the situation!

One sure method for managing the audience is to use the SEE factor:

- *Spontaneity:* Respond immediately to issues of concern or concepts that need clarification.

- *Enthusiasm:* Be genuinely glad to be facilitating the learning situation; welcome their questions or queries. If the time or issue is not appropriate when it is presented, agree on a mutual time or forum for discussion (use the so-called parking lot technique for placing an issue someplace until you can get to it).

- *Eye contact:* Be an active listener by looking at the person talking with you, and be an active presenter by focusing on the members of your audience. Don't look over their heads, at your notes, the flipcharts, or visual aids: Talk to them. Be engaging.

Teaching is holding a conversation. Provide a structure for the conversation and direct the dialogue so that it is open and satisfying for the learning and for you, the trainer.

Watch Your Time

Your time limit is a contract between you and your audience. The two most important clauses of the contract are starting on time and ending on time.

When you were planning, preparing, and rehearsing your presentation, you paid attention to time. More than likely you devoted appropriate time to each segment. When you plan for one full day or more, be realistic about your timing. Design in minutes for each hour. Five minutes within each 60 minutes is for the learners to settle in. There are six hours of training time per day, not eight. And there are breaks! We are now discovering in learning-brain research that learners need to take mental breaks every 20 minutes and physical breaks every 50 minutes. Allocate your time according to your major points.

When you are making your delivery, trust yourself. If the time allocation does not seem appropriate as you proceed in your presentation, make adjustments.

Plan the Question and Answer Session

Most presentations build a question and answer session into the end. This session allows the conversation you are having to move in directions the trainees might want to go. Plan ahead by having answers to questions that your various rehearsal audiences might have asked or that you anticipate this audience might ask.

What do you do if the unthinkable happens, and no one is asking a question? You have several options:

- You can avoid the appearance of no questions by planting a colleague or two in the audience who will ask questions. Sometimes that one question will encourage other people to start asking.

- You can ask a question yourself: "Someone once asked me..."

- You can end the presentation gracefully: "Seeing that there are no questions, let's end for today."

Audiences have a variety of reasons for asking questions. Don't assume that all those who ask questions are seeking information. People may ask questions to test you, show their own knowledge, make points, or get your approval. Your ability to manage questions and questioners is important to the success of your delivery. Following are some tips for managing your audience during the question and answer session:

- Receive all questions in an open, friendly manner. Don't react or be defensive, even if someone is trying to put you on the spot.

- Listen carefully and restate the question to make sure you understand it and the entire audience hears it.

- Think before you answer. Consider the following processing points before providing a response:
  — Why is someone asking this question?
  — How does this question fit with my purpose?
  — How can I answer as briefly and as well as possible?

Use the KISS principle: Keep It Simple and Succinct. However, do not answer simply yes or no; answer with a short, to-the-point statement, perhaps supported by a brief example.

- Admit to not knowing an answer and offer to find out the answer and then follow up with the answer.

Close With Conviction
Use body language to indicate that you have finished your presentation. Nod, and step back briskly from your speaking position.

Merely saying, "Thank you," is too short and too often reveals the unspoken and felt, "Thank God that's over." Use SEE—spontaneity, enthusiasm, and eye contact—especially enthusiasm, to help you close with conviction. You might close with words such as, "I enjoyed being with you. Thank you for your attention and your participation. Best of luck to all of you."

Exit a Winner

When you are planning, organizing, and rehearsing your presentation, be sure to include how you will leave the speaking area as well as what you will do immediately upon leaving the area. You have several options:

- to sit in the chair from which you were introduced
- to stand on stage to greet people
- to move around the room to greet people
- to go into the hall to greet people
- to leave the area so that the group can proceed to another activity.

You want to manage your audience in the last moment the same way you managed them in the first moment and throughout the delivery: professionally. Leave the way you entered: briskly, firmly, and confidently. Remember that although you may no longer be holding a conversation, you are "on" until you are out of sight.

SUMMARY AND HIGHLIGHTS

Following are key points to remember when you prepare to implement your presentation:

- Delivery is holding a conversation with your audience.
- The most important and time-consuming step is planning the delivery.
- Conduct research to help you know your audience and the venue in which you will be making your presentation.
- Selecting materials and the format for your delivery requires understanding the relationship of your content to the type of training you will be conducting.
- Organizing the presentation forces you to decide whether you will use the theory session or the skill session model and to plan the body, the conclusion, and the introduction, in that order.

- Creating the presentation provides the opportunity to think about what words you will use, what type of visual aids will best support your words and your message, how to benefit from editing your script and rehearsing your presentation, and how to put the best of your personality into your presentation.
- The following tips can help you create effective visual aids.
  — Use large type or letters.
  — Write clearly.
  — Limit the number of ideas per chart and focus on key words or ideas.
  — Remember the seven-seven rule.
  — Explain, amplify, or give examples of the words on the visual aid.
  — Use a progression technique—expose one idea at a time— for particularly complicated visual aids.
- Managing your audience is merely paying attention to the group with whom you are engaged in conversation, which is best done by fulfilling your contract to delivery on time and in the allotted time.

Use the presentation checklist in table 3 by mentally or physically checking off each stage of the presentation as you go through the day.

Consider monitoring the progress of your presentation by use of summarizing questions or a checklist on a flipchart or learning map that depicts the major elements of the presentation. If you use a wall chart or learning map, make sure you refer to each element on it. If you use a visual checklist, make sure you check off the segments you complete. The presentation checklist is for you, the trainer, to keep track of your topic and your timing. Develop a mechanism that works best for you. You can share your checklist with the audience if you so choose.

Remember the following rules:

1. Write talking notes in pencil.
2. Change colors in your talking notes for visual interest and relief.

Table 3. Presentation checklist.	
ITEM	**DATE COMPLETED**
Accept invitation to deliver training.	
Write title.	
Determine purpose.	
Prepare instructional objectives.	
Identify your audience.	
Learn about the physical setting in which you will deliver training.	
Research the content.	
Organize your material and determine the exact content.	
Plan the body.	
Plan the conclusion.	
Plan the introduction.	
Decide which delivery method you will use.	
Create the presentation.	
Plan the visual aids.	
Engage a full-service shop to execute the visual aids.	
Receive professionally prepared visual aids.	
Type your notes.	
Rehearse for yourself.	
Rehearse for others.	
Conduct a dress rehearsal.	

3. Underline your talking notes for clarity.

4. Underline your talking notes for emphasis

The next chapter, evaluation, will give you the final pieces you need so you can put a well-prepared and tested training program to work.

7

Evaluation

Evaluation is closely entwined with implementation. But before you can even deliver the program, you need a plan. You must consider three critical points: how to structure the training event, how to implement the training, and how to evaluate the training.

STRUCTURING THE TRAINING EVENT

The training event consists of three critical phases: the pretraining stage, learning stage, and after-training stage. No matter how appropriate or effective your design, training technique, or training facility may be, learning takes place only if the training is structured properly. In his book *Human Resource Management,* Randall S. Schuler (1996) lists the following critical factors to address at each phase of the training:

- Phase 1: Setting the Stage for Learning
  - Provide clear task instructions.
  - Model appropriate behavior.
  - Communicate management support.

- Phase 2: Increasing Learning During Training
  - Provide for active participation.
  - Match training techniques to trainees' abilities.

— Provide opportunities for mastery practice.

— Ensure specific, timely, diagnostic, and practical feedback.

- Phase 3: Maintaining Performance After Training

  — Develop learning points to assist in knowledge retention.

  — Set specific goals.

  — Identify appropriate reinforcers.

  — Train others in how to reinforce behavior.

  — Teach self-management skills to trainees.

During training, take the needed steps to increase knowledge and skill retention and conclude the training event with specific strategies that learners can use to transfer the training successfully to the job.

IMPLEMENTING THE TRAINING

Managing the implementation stages of the training event is a complex but necessary process. Here are some guidelines to the implementation process that Rosemary Brehm and I developed for the American Management Association. It is important to cover the following topics with instructors or facilitators:

- instructor guide
- methods to measure consistency, instructor readiness, and ongoing performance
- accountability of the instructor to meet objectives.

With learners, it's important to cover:

- accountability to perform in training
- feedback systems
- training transfer systems.

With administration, it's important to cover the following materials and logistical requirements:

- precourse materials
- classroom materials
- practices
- test items
- evaluations

- hands-on materials
- hardware, software
- simulations, job-related materials
- postcourse materials
- location and facilities
- training sites, rooms, break-out rooms
- technical and audiovisual needs
- hotel and restaurant facilities
- multi-site locations
- course registration and confirmation procedures.

A fourth implementation area that is often overlooked is management. You need management's support for your training to be successful. This support develops in an organization that promotes a learning organization philosophy. It also comes when providing resources to transfer training from classroom to the job.

How well management supports the learner and the instructor has an impact on training. If management does not encourage course participation and follow up on the job, then training will not succeed.

Training will succeed if management acts as a visible and vocal sponsor for training, the instructor, and the training process to support training job skills transfer.

EVALUATING THE TRAINING

You evaluate your training program in order to measure the effectiveness of the training. Evaluation allows you to determine the effectiveness and efficiency of your training program through the design and delivery stages. The purpose of evaluation is to:

- determine if training is meeting its stated goals and objectives
- determine if the implementation of the training program is practical
- determine if the learners are meeting established performance criteria
- provide necessary feedback so that the training program can be maintained.

To accomplish these goals, evaluation activities must occur throughout the training program.

Evaluation and the Design Process

Evaluation is a vital part of any training program, and instructional design is incomplete without it. Planning for evaluation should take place before the program activities are designed.

Evaluation is a significant part of the instructional design and delivery process, not just an element in program outcomes. As part of the program development process, evaluation can help programs succeed and can stop ill-conceived or poorly executed programs from happening.

It is important to plan the evaluation process early in the design stage in order to establish the mechanisms for assessing the ongoing effect of the training, rather than to wait to assess the impact after program delivery.

Evaluation Models and Design Process

All evaluation models contain these characteristics: They identify evaluation goals, develop an evaluation design and strategy, select and construct measurement tools, and analyze data.

There are four primary approaches to evaluation, according to Hannum and Hansen (1989), each of which has a different use and intent. The decision-making model is to collect evaluation data for the purpose of informing decision makers about the effectiveness of a training program. The accreditation model focuses on the use of professional judgment and processes to assess the work of an educational or training program. The goal-based evaluation model attempts to determine the extent to which the educational or training program meets its stated goals. The purpose of a goal-based model is to determine the trainees' degree of goal attainment. In the goal-free evaluation model, the evaluator attempts to document the effects of an education or training program, not to measure progress toward predetermined goals.

Five Levels of Evaluation

Another approach to evaluation is the performance-based training (PBT) model that Marshall and Schriver (1994) developed. PBT requires that a trainee demonstrate both knowledge and skills before leaving training.

Consider using the following five-step model, which is similar to PBT, to separate knowledge and skills. The five levels are as follows:

1. *Self:* As a trainer, you need feedback. Trainers often overlook the need to conduct self-analysis feedback, but you need to take the time to reflect on your performance, to ask yourself what went well, what did not go so well, and what you might need to change. In addition to your own insight, you can receive feedback from trainees' evaluation forms and colleagues' feedback. Questions you could use in any of the situations to start a dialogue might include: Could I have done better? What are areas for improvement?

2. *Course materials:* The materials are usually designed in a one-dimensional written format. You don't know how the written notes and suggested processes are going to evolve until the training takes place. Therefore, the learners' comments, written trainees' evaluation critique, and your observations in the training session provide you with the needed feedback. Questions might include: Does the material work? Are there portions that are difficult to deliver? Do learners exhibit difficulty with materials or training situations? Do courses or training processes need revising or updating?

3. *Course curriculum:* Like the course materials, the course curriculum is prepared on paper. The implementation phase allows you to test your design by getting feedback during the training delivery process. Your feedback would, therefore, come from yourself, learners, or observers. Questions might include: Does the course curriculum hang together? Does the course meet the intended learning objectives and outcomes?

4. *Course modules:* Just as with the course materials and course design, the course modules are your written interpretation of what you should deliver. Your feedback consists of a self-analysis of the course modules, your experience during the delivery stage, and reactions from learners or observers. Questions might include: Are the modules organized around a theoretical theme? Are the topics sequenced in logical order? Does each module contribute to the course outcomes and learning objectives?

5. *Learning transfer:* Both written and oral feedback about the transfer of learning to the workplace is important during the training event and as a posttraining activity. Questions might include: How effective was the transfer of learning to each learner's work situation? How effective is the learning transfer to the real world of work?

Evaluation Designs

Jack Phillips (1991), one of my contemporaries in the field of evaluation, states that a critical issue to resolve is how to evaluate. Some of the most common design methods are a one-shot program, single-group pretest and posttest, single-group time series, and control group design.

Let's first consider the one-shot-program design for evaluation of a single group after completion of a training program. In this design, no data are collected prior to the program. Many uncontrolled factors, such as the environment (time of day and place) and the trainees' attitudes (energy level, learners' accomplishments, their perceived ability to transfer the learned concepts and, finally, their attitude about the training event) might influence the design's measurement and invalidate conclusions drawn from it.

There are two situations in which this design may be useful: when measuring the performance of a group for which it was not possible to measure performance beforehand, and when there is no significant knowledge, skill, or ability existing before the program is conducted.

The single-group pretest and posttest design goes one step beyond the one-shot design by collecting data before and after the training program. To detect improvements, the learners' knowledge, skills, or abilities before the program is compared with their knowledge, skills, or abilities after the program. The disadvantage of the pretest strategy is that it may sensitize learners to the training content, which might affect the posttest.

A single-group time series design is a series of measurements for evaluating training programs before and after the program. In this design, the experimental group serves as its own control group. The multiple measurements prior to the program eliminate the problems incurred when a separate control group is not used. Repeated measurements after the program allow for comparison of the initial results and enable measurement of the program's long-term effects.

The control group design compares two groups, one experimental and one control. The experimental group receives the training program, whereas the control group does not. Data are gathered on both groups before and after the program. Comparing the results of the experimental group to the control group assesses the impact of the training program. For this design to be acceptable, the two groups must be similar with respect to the selection criteria.

Decisions Around Evaluation

An effective evaluation is essential to improve a program and demonstrate its value. One of the important considerations is when to evaluate. In the 1993 interview my class held with Nadler, which I mentioned in chapter 5, he said he believes evaluation should be performed frequently and throughout a lesson. Particularly crucial points, he said, are when a main topic has been completed or when a full understanding of a main topic must be evaluated before moving on to the next lesson or module.

Nadler's critical events model provides for an ongoing evaluation and feedback mechanism. The evaluation and feedback process is necessary to ensure that the activities are directly related to the needs of the learners or decision makers, says Nadler. Evaluations assess both the outcomes of the training program and the components of instructional design and development.

Suggestions from Mel Silberman (1990) provide a further understanding of evaluation. Silberman suggests that evaluation efforts should address what is happening in a training program and the possible effects on learning and the learner. He suggests a similar evaluation process to Nadler's. It involves inquiry and decision making throughout the design and development processes. Silberman suggests making decisions in the following areas:

- *The elements to be evaluated.* Data can be gathered concerning any of the following elements in program content and design; trainer's competence; learner's knowledge, skills, and attitudes; training facilities; and organizational results.

- *The tools to be used to collect evaluative data.* They may include: questionnaires, observation, tests, reports, and interviews.

- *The timing for data collection.* Data collection may occur during pretraining, training, the end of training, and the follow-up period.

Two Categories of Evaluation

There are two categories of evaluation, each one of which provides different information to ensure the training is on track. The first category of evaluation, program evaluation, assesses the impact of a training program on learning. The second category of evaluation, training transfer evaluation, measures the success of the learner's ability to transfer the learning back on the job.

Program Evaluation

There are two types of evaluation processes for measuring a training program's effectiveness, formative and summative. Formative evaluation activities occur throughout the business justification, analysis, design, development, and implementation stages to identify required revisions.

Summative evaluation activities occur at the end of training program delivery to determine if the training met the goals and objectives. Summative evaluation can include, for example, performance-based evaluation, follow-up or longitudinal evaluation, and program effectiveness evaluation.

Table 1 can assist you in deciding which evaluation process you should use to measure program effectiveness.

When you conduct a program evaluation, keep in mind that a good quality evaluation consists of a comprehensive data-collection effort and a

Table 1. Types of evaluation processes.

TYPE	DESCRIPTION	METHOD
Formative	Type of evaluation that assesses program before full implementation. Instructional designer usually conducts with smaller focus groups.	Test materials and instructional methods at each phase of the development.
Summative	Type of evaluation that assesses the final training program or product after implementation (usually with Kirkpatrick's level model).	Determine degree to which objectives were met and the results after widespread use of training.

consistent and conscientious attempt to revise instructional materials on the basis of these data.

Feedback Loop to the Instructional Systems Design Model

During the design and development process, it is essential that you continually check back to the program objectives and test items that you prepared as a first step in this instructional systems design (ISD) process. Remember, the ISD model establishes the blueprint for the design and development of your training intervention. The model dictates the sequential steps involved in developing your training.

Evaluation results usually indicate the area to be revised. Revisions could be in the area of timing, content, activities, or course materials. The materials may be handouts, participant workbooks, overheads, or wall charts. Once you've identified one or more areas to be revised, you can determine the appropriate step for revision in the training system model by checking your data against the model. For example, if an objective statement is faulty, the revision would start at the analysis stage. Or, the trainer might suggest that the content covered in the training program or the activities that were designed and developed to meet the learning objective might need to be addressed to meet the learners' needs or, more specifically, the defined learning outcome.

If a module is poorly organized, then the revision starts at the development stage. In many cases, evaluation will include an analysis of end users' interaction with newly learned skills.

To test the effectiveness of training, such as the use of a job aid, you will want to observe how well users can perform selected tasks. By conducting this step, you can provide valuable feedback to the training designer. For example, users' problems may reflect a poorly designed software interface rather than a poorly designed job aid.

In these situations, the ultimate goal is to use the evaluation process as a vehicle to identify how the software may be improved, thereby reducing or eliminating the need for training.

Training Transfer Evaluation

Transfer of training is the effective and continuing on-the-job application of knowledge and skills gained in training—both on and off the job, according to Broad and Newstrom (1992). Although learning is the planned outcome of any training intervention, the most important critical events for any training intervention is to have the learner transfer the new skills, knowledge, and abilities to the job.

Learning transfer can occur in a variety of ways. Donald L. Kirkpatrick developed one of the most popular models. In his book *Evaluating Training Programs: The Four Levels,* Kirkpatrick (1994) identifies the following four levels at which training can be evaluated:

- Level 1, learner reaction (attitude or feeling regarding satisfaction and dissatisfaction with the training)
- Level 2, learner test (observable or measurable behavior change in the classroom or training situation)
- Level 3, behavior transfer (new or changed behavior; performance back on the job)
- Level 4, organizational impact (for example, increased productivity, sales quality, or reduction in costs, accidents, grievances due to appropriate training that addressed the identified need).

At Level 1, you evaluate a learner's reaction. Reaction sheets, or happy sheets, are the most popular mechanism for conducting this evaluation. This evaluation only measures how a person feels about the training, that is, happy or not happy.

At Level 2, you evaluate a learner's mastery of the program content by using a test. This evaluation only measures the learner's ability to answer test questions.

At Level 3, you evaluate a learner's ability to transfer the learning on the job. This evaluation is difficult to accomplish unless you have had prior discussions with the learner's supervisor and manager, and they agreed that certain mastery should occur in the learning and that the successful transfer of the training will be reported back.

At Level 4, you evaluate the organizational impact of the training. This evaluation can only be accomplished if a well-defined training issue that affected the organization was identified and the training targeted the issue.

Table 2 describes the level, the type of evaluation, and the key questions to be addressed.

But how do you get from the four levels of evaluation to designing and conducting the course? Let's consider evaluation methods. Table 3 shows

LEVEL	EVALUATES	DESCRIPTION
1	Learner reaction	How did the learner react to the course?
2	Learning	How well did the learner apply the new skills and knowledge during the course?
3	Training transfer	What changes in job behavior resulted from the training?
4	Organizational impact	What were the results of training on the company's bottom line?

Table 2. Evaluating successful training transfer.

you for each of Kirkpatrick's levels when to measure, what to measure, and how to measure for successful learning transfer. The premise of Kirkpatrick's evaluation model is that these four levels can be used to design and test how successful you were as a trainer in presenting the information for the learner to master. In the role of the trainer, however, you can only manage and test successful transfer at Levels 1 and 2. Once you begin to assess the success of learning transfer at Level 3, you must include the learner's supervisor or manager, or both, back on the job. When you want to test the level of successful transfer at Level 4, organizational impact, you first must start with a well-defined needs assessment statement, which defines a need that has a significant impact on the organization and shows training as the solution to the defined need. Once the training has occurred, you can test to determine the impact training had on that need.

Table 3. Evaluation worksheet.

LEVEL	WHEN TO MEASURE	WHAT TO MEASURE	MEASURE USED INSTRUMENT
1	During program (end of day) End of program	Reactions Pace and sequence Relevance (content) Instrument strategies Interaction Facilitators' style Level of discussion Objectives met Environment Knowledge of facilitator Participant interaction Registration process	Questionnaire Individual responses in class Follow-up interviews
2	During the program Pre and post (end)	Is learning taking place, and to what extent? Teaching of content Knowledge of participants	Knowledge tests Performance tests, role plays, case studies Checklists Product tests
3	After the program A few weeks to three months	On-the-job change	Performance records Performance contracts Action plans Interviews Observation with checklists
4	After the program Three months to one year	Impact on organization	Action plans Interviews Questionnaires Focus groups Performance contract
5	After the program Three months to one year	Determine monetary value of impact	Control groups Trend line Participants' estimates Supervisors' estimates Management's estimate Use of experts Extant data External studies

Source: Adapted with permission from Donald V. McCain, Ed.D., Performance Advantage Group, Brentwood, TN; 615.377.3050.

To measure how well trainees absorbed material covered in your training program, take advantage of a variety of assessment tools. The most effective assessment methods are checklists, questionnaires, and interviews.

Checklists allow trainers or facilitators, managers, and trainees to assign value to different training topics. The disadvantage of checklists is that answers are subjective, and, as such, not necessarily valid.

Questionnaires are used when evaluation time is limited and cost is a primary concern. Questionnaires can reach a large number of people and can investigate levels of knowledge, analyze skills, and elicit attitudes. Properly formatted questionnaires provide data for relatively easy statistical analysis. The disadvantages are that responses are subjective, there are difficulties constructing easy-to-understand questions, and there are problems trying to produce a valid and reliable format.

Interviews can be used with trainers or facilitators, managers, and learners. The interview process can elicit information such as personal impressions about the quality of training and differences in performance. The disadvantages are that interviews are often time-consuming and expensive to design, conduct, and analyze.

Table 4 shows the advantages and disadvantages of a variety of evaluation methods.

METHODS TO MEASURE LEARNING

To measure learning, it's helpful to use experimental methods. Experiments may be set up in several different ways. People trained in experimental design and statistics are often needed to conduct these studies and interpret the results. The results indicate the effectiveness of the training from an objective viewpoint. The following three types of methods yield information on learning:

- *Postmeasure:* This type of test consists of training a group of employees and then assessing what they have learned and how they performed on the job. However, this method cannot determine whether trainees' knowledge or skill levels have changed, much less attribute the changes to the training experience. Even if trainees perform well on the posttest, this finding could reflect their previous skill levels, not necessarily be an effect of training.

Table 4. Guidelines for evaluating learning.

STRATEGIES	ADVANTAGES	DISADVANTAGES
Written tests/assessments (could be pre/post)	√ Provides documentation √ Immediate feedback √ Knowledge reinforcement √ Easy to administer √ Flexibility in timing √ Advanced organizer √ Reinforces knowledge content	√ Creates anxiety/stress √ Difficult to construct √ Legal implications
Performance tests/assessments	√ Allows for self-discovery √ Allows for application √ Can be an instructional strategy (case study, role play, etc.) √ Reinforces course content and skills √ Immediate feedback √ Behaviorally oriented √ Simulates the job	√ Requires time √ Legal implications √ Training of observers/assessors √ More can affect performance than training (pre-training skills)
Skill test/assessment	√ Replicates the job √ Separates levels of dexterity √ Supports job standards √ Immediate feedback √ Allows for direct application of knowledge and skills √ Reinforces skills	√ Determining level of performance √ Legal implications √ Availability of equipment √ Availability of equipment room √ Training of observers/assessors
Work product test/assessment	√ Replicates the job √ Allows for direct application of knowledge and skills √ Links to field supervisors/leads √ Supports job/product standards √ Subject Matter Expert involvement √ Reinforces skills	√ Availability of equipment √ Disruptive to work environment √ High visibility/Higher risk √ Legal implications √ Time consuming √ May take equipment out of service impacting production √ Training of observers/assessors √ May be difficult to construct and assess

Source: Adapted with permission from Donald V. McCain, Ed.D., Performance Advantage Group, Brentwood, TN; 615.377.3050.

- *Pre- and postmeasures:* Pretests and posttests alleviate some of the guesswork associated with posttest-only designs by establishing a baseline of knowledge or skill level prior to training. Once employees have received training, a second level of knowledge or skill is obtained, and the two sets of scores are compared to determine improvement. Intervening variables other than training may influence the posttest scores.

- *Pre- and postmeasures with control group:* Using this method, two groups have their performances evaluated. Then one group participates in training, but the other group does not. After training, the performance of both groups is reevaluated to determine if the group that received the training performs significantly better than the group that did not receive training. A possible pitfall of this method is that training group members may interact with control group members and "teach" them what they learned during the training.

METHODS TO MEASURE BEHAVIOR

Changes in behavior can be evaluated using a variety of methods. Combining the methods may yield the truest picture of behavioral changes. Methods for evaluating behavior include performance tests, critical incidents, multirater 360 feedback, simulations, observations, and performance appraisals.

Performance tests contain actual samples of content taught in the training program. This type of test measures behavior changes that transfer to the work environment.

Critical incidents record significant positive and negative incidents to measure training outcome. An employee's supervisor usually conducts this evaluation. The method measures positive and negative behaviors well, but midrange behaviors are difficult to quantify.

Multirater 360 feedback, which is described further below, evaluates performance using self, peers, direct reports, management, and other relevant perspectives, such as those of customers and suppliers.

Simulations provide an experiential bridge between training and its real-world context. How well the trainee performs the simulation can be a measurement of training effectiveness. Simulations that reflect the work environment accurately can be expensive to construct.

Observations assess complex performance that is difficult to assess by means of a questionnaire, interview, or simulation. A problem with this technique is that it must be properly structured for quantitative data collection. An observation checklist is organized to list categories and frequency of behavior to be observed. The checklist becomes the instrument used to help quantify performance.

In most cases, management depends on evaluation results to determine the effectiveness of training. Information about results can be determined from performance appraisals, progress toward organizational objectives, and the multirater 360 feedback process.

Performance appraisals evaluate how well employees measure up to various performance standards. During a performance appraisal, the supervisor compares the actual performance to the performance standards and judges whether skills taught in training are practiced in the workshop.

Progress toward organizational objectives will tell management whether training is working well. Training should advance the company toward its mission. If the bottom line is improving, management may approve more funding for training. If the company isn't closer to meeting its objectives, training may be viewed as ineffective.

The 360-feedback process can involve a multiple-customer approach. Traditional performance management systems focused on one-way feedback, supervisor to employee. Business initiatives such as total quality management, teams, and reengineering have resulted in an additional focus on customers and added value. In response to these needs, many organizations have implemented 360-feedback systems, although other organizations have reservations about these systems. One criticism is that the process involves more people and takes more time and money to execute than most other evaluation methods. Critics also say that people rating the employee may not understand the total job requirements and environment. In addition, some critics say that the potential benefits of 360-feedback systems are still unproven.

Keep in mind, however, that when multirater systems are well implemented, they provide feedback to the employees from the supervisors, peers, direct reports, the team, and customers (internal and external). When such systems are based upon core competencies, they ultimately support the vision and values of the organization and the changing shape of the organization, the expectations of employees, and the increasing level in interdependence throughout the organization to achieve desired goals.

EVALUATION EFFECTIVENESS

For evaluation to be effective, several things must be present. First, evaluation must be linked to the needs analysis to determine present and anticipated problems and opportunities.

Second, the feedback must be timely. The evaluation data must be given to the appropriate people while the training program and potential problems are still current.

Third, evaluation data must be collected on an ongoing basis throughout the training process, summarized right after the training, and acted upon immediately.

Fourth, the training environment must support change. The effectiveness of an evaluation system is contingent upon a training environment that allows change. An environment not supportive of change could result in a situation in which trainers are not obligated to improve training; lack the time, knowledge, or skills required to change the training; or lack management support for effective change.

Data Collection

Ongoing data collection is essential for ensuring evaluation effectiveness. The data document changes in performance, instructors' effectiveness, learning, impact, and the like. Interviews, observations, questionnaires, and tests provide information you use in establishing a baseline, or benchmark, with which to make design decisions. This baseline information can then provide the basis for a discussion with management about the need for a training intervention.

Once you collect your information and share it with management, management must then decide on the value of the training. Trainers and the instructional designer should help in interpreting the data and in suggesting ways to correct any problems that turn up in the performance study. Here are some guidelines for collecting, managing, validating, and ensuring that your evaluation processes are appropriate and correct.

There are two basic kinds or categories of data, hard and soft, as described in chapter 3. The primary measurement of improvement is hard data, which are presented as rational, undisputed facts. The ultimate criteria for measuring the effectiveness of management rest on hard data items such as return-on-investment, productivity, profitability, cost control, and quality control. Because changes in the data lag behind changes in the condition of the human organization, it is very useful to supplement these measures with interim assessments of attitude, motivation, satisfaction, and skills. These soft data items are more difficult to collect and analyze but are used when hard data are not available.

Types of Measurement

There are four basis tactics for measuring results: experimental, critical incident, problem solving, and management information systems (MIS).

The experimental approach emphasizes comparing trained and untrained, or pre- and posttrained learners (or some combination of both) on several predetermined measures of performance. After a reasonable period of time, the results are compared by using a descriptive statistical process. Because there are so many possible variables, both positive and negative correlations can occur by chance, especially if only a single outcome is being measured. The consequence is that you can't necessarily rely on statistical results to prove your program's impact.

The critical incident approach requires the trainer to solicit and collect specific incidents or stories of improved performance from the trained population to show the effectiveness of the training effort. With this approach, a lot of evaluative information is generated, and if done in a systematic and logical way, you can continuously tie results to program objectives.

With the problem-solving approach, the trainer is involved in identifying, quantifying, and solving high-priority problems, and the contribution to profits is easily measured. High-priority problems easily lend themselves to pre- and postmeasurement and provide high visibility. If training programs are based on clear objectives that have been developed by careful needs analysis and are directly related to profit-producing performance or behavior, then the results of training will invariably be quantifiable.

The management information system approach holds that looking at the impact of training should be part of an ongoing performance tracking and feedback system. Tracking and feedback should include attitude, after-training performance, and ongoing progress reports.

Basic Models for Data Collection

There are three basic models for data collection: preexperimental, true experimental, and quasi-experimental. The preexperimental model doesn't adhere to the tenets of basic experimental design. A common example is an evaluation that consists of only one group that participated in a training program and then was evaluated without being compared with another group. One way to improve the method would be to test learners before and after the training program, because that would reduce one source of possible evaluation error. There remains the problem of attributing to the training program the results of the test. The single-group posttest only and the single-group pretest, posttest are both considered preexperimental models.

True experimental models have a comparison group that is equivalent to the training group because each person is assigned to a group by a random process. Random assignment increases the probability that the groups are equivalent in every way except that only one group participates in the training program. The problem with implementing a true experimental model is the difficulty with random assignment and the problem of withholding the instruction from the comparison group.

The quasi-experimental designs differ from the true experimental designs in that they don't have random assignment to the training group and comparison groups. One commonly used quasi-experimental model has two groups that are not assigned at random, but that are constituted to be as close as is feasible. Another possible quasi-experimental model uses multiple measures on one group over time. In this approach, the evaluator takes several performance measures before the training program begins, and then takes several measures after its completion and examines the data for trends.

Validity and Reliability

Data-collection information must be valid and reliable, which requires sound development and use of the instruments. According to Jack Phillips (1994), there are four ways to determine if an instrument is valid: content, construct, concurrent, and predictive validity.

First, the extent to which the instrument represents the content of the program is content validity. Low-content validity means the instrument does not represent a true summation of the program content. High-content validity means the instrument represents a good balance of all the program content.

Construct validity refers to the degree to which an instrument represents the construct it is supposed to measure. The abstract variable that the instrument is intended to measure, such as the skill, attitude, or ability, is the construct. Construct validity can be defended through expert opinion, correlations, logical deductions, and criterion group studies.

Concurrent validity is the extent to which an instrument agrees with the results of other instruments administered at approximately the same time to measure the same characteristics.

The extent to which an instrument can predict future behaviors or results is predictive validity.

A reliable survey instrument is one that is consistent enough that subsequent measurements of an item give approximately the same results. A test or survey is considered reliable if it yields consistent results at two different points in time. This assumes that there have been no major changes in people or circumstances and no intervening treatments.

System for Tracking Results

From my perspective during the past five years—as a human resource manager and instructional designer who's been teaching instructional design at Johns Hopkins University, Radcliffe College, and the American Management Association as well as designing training for the Internet at Florida Gulf Coast University—I've concluded that trainers must develop a system to monitor results.

After the program's outcomes have been clearly delineated, it is important to design a system that will monitor the results achieved both in qualitative and quantitative terms. The outcomes to be tracked are to be mutually agreed upon by the client and the trainer. The system must then track both on-the-job behavior change and the bottom-line impact to the organization.

The survey process must be created, and it should include establishing a baseline of performance for comparisons. This requires collecting behavioral information both prior to training and following the training. It also may be appropriate to compare the performance of trainees with the performance of a similar group of people not receiving the training.

Tracking data at all four of Kirkpatrick's levels of evaluation is important especially if return-on-investment (ROI) is an organizational focus. Tracking progress in terms of dollar payback against dollar objectives will add control to the training.

Evaluation is critical to the success of the design, development, and delivery of coursework and of field implementation of the new skills and behaviors. The evaluation strategy includes linking evaluation to the entire design process and developing the instruments to conduct the actual evaluation. The individuals involved in the evaluation process must be identified and included in the evaluation effort. The feedback is then used to enhance the quality of the program or, in some cases, to halt the effort.

Finally, once you determine that the request for training is truly a training issue, Kirkpatrick's four levels of evaluation should be addressed during the initial needs assessment phase. To guarantee that training transfer will take place, you must define and develop your evaluation mechanism early.

Level 1 evaluation can be improved by having learners weight the objectives according to their perception of each objective's importance prior to the program. At the conclusion of the program, participants then indicate the extent to which the objectives were achieved. By multiplying the weight by the achievement, you receive more accurate feedback.

A Level 2 evaluation should include both knowledge and application. Knowledge tests can be developed along more traditional testing formats. The application of the knowledge can be evaluated by using behavioral checklists to evaluate learner performance on simulations, case studies, or problem-based learning exercises.

A Level 3 evaluation should include a behavioral checklist indicating the degree to which the learned knowledge and behavior change are being implemented in the field. A manager could be identified to be the person to complete the checklist on the basis of his or her observation. Interviews should also be conducted with program participants to determine the factors involved in the skill transfer and to identify what helped or hindered their application of the new knowledge, skills, and behaviors back on the job. Another method would be to conduct 360 feedback. The first 360-feedback evaluation would be to establish a benchmark. After completion of a training and development plan, a second 360 feedback would be conducted. Then, you would compare the second 360 with the benchmark data to see if change has taken place.

At Level 4 evaluation, you will probably provide correlation rather than causality. One possibility to determine change is to have a well-defined training need at the outset that affects the entire organization, say customer service satisfaction. The training provided corrects a dysfunctional customer service process. Complaints go way down, and sales could increase. One might suggest this is due to retraining. Or you could compare these data with those of other customer service professionals, for example, who have not taken the training.

END NOTE

Because human beings yearn for knowledge, new skills, and abilities, training plays an integral role in satisfying these needs, strengthening confidence, and building competence. My experience over the years as an organizational development and training specialist has shown me that if people see a need for training in their job or work or if a real need for knowing something exists, they'll learn what they need even under the most difficult conditions.

I recall a woman who worked in the food-service industry who knew what the training needs were in her department but knew nothing about training, or so she thought. After toiling for many hours, she developed a proposal, with some guidance from me, and presented it to her supervisors. The next day management approved her proposal and slated her as the trainer.

Although this example is outside the norm, it illustrates the importance of creativity and spontaneity in developing a training program as well as the role motivation plays. Much of this book presents the process for you, the training professional, to use to design situations to assist the people who want to learn. Those who want to learn are motivated!

This awareness has made me more careful about who attends a training session. Once I've made sure that the people who attend the training want to learn, then I can direct my energies to providing a quality presentation.

If you could take away just one thought from this book, it would be to consider the importance of planning and ferreting out the real need for training. People will act or react according to how they are rewarded. I now spend much of my design and development time working with clients to establish if a need for training exists, and, if so, the real intent of training. And if change is wanted, we agree on how much and in what direction. To do otherwise simply frustrates the learners and often makes less of an opportunity.

NOTES

Some material for this chapter is based on the Society for Human Resource Management Learning System Certification Guide (1997). For more information about the certification program, contact SHRM, 1800 Duke St., Alexandria, VA 22314; 703.548.3440; www.shrm.org

Don McCain from Performance Advantage Group provided me with this summary of contemporary models and processes for this publication.

Tool Kit
Tips and Techniques

Chapter 1 introduced you to the training system model (see figure 1). This tool of the trade is a step-by-step guide for designing and developing successful training interventions. By taking training one step at a time, the trainer or designer can be sure that the training intervention is appropriately designed and meets the need of the learners and the sponsoring organization.

CONSULTING AND CONTRACTING   TIP #1

Being a training consultant is not just a title. You are a business. Being in the training business requires planning, marketing, and financial management. Being a professional training consultant means that you are in this business full time, not just until you can find a so-called real job. Training consulting is a real job, and, generally speaking, running a training business is more demanding than many other so-called real jobs.

Tips on Consulting

Before you begin your consulting business, examine the market around you. Try and find a niche. Determine if the industry has a need for your services and if it is willing to pay for you to perform a service that you

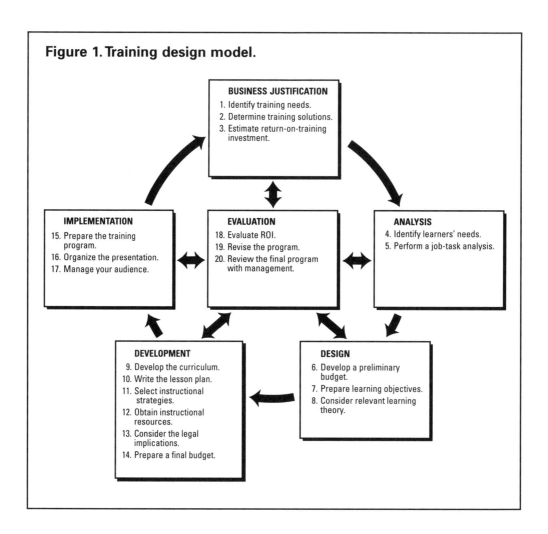

Figure 1. Training design model.

BUSINESS JUSTIFICATION
1. Identify training needs.
2. Determine training solutions.
3. Estimate return-on-training investment.

IMPLEMENTATION
15. Prepare the training program.
16. Organize the presentation.
17. Manage your audience.

EVALUATION
18. Evaluate ROI.
19. Revise the program.
20. Review the final program with management.

ANALYSIS
4. Identify learners' needs.
5. Perform a job-task analysis.

DEVELOPMENT
9. Develop the curriculum.
10. Write the lesson plan.
11. Select instructional strategies.
12. Obtain instructional resources.
13. Consider the legal implications.
14. Prepare a final budget.

DESIGN
6. Develop a preliminary budget.
7. Prepare learning objectives.
8. Consider relevant learning theory.

can provide. At first, you'll probably perform a variety of duties until you decide that you have found a niche. Finally, finding your niche takes time, research, thought, marketing, and trial and error. Eventually you will carve a unique market share for your business. This share doesn't always have to be a unique product that you have developed. It could be that you develop a clientele based purely on the way you do business.

Realistic evaluation of your ability to reach potential customers is important. Having a network of people is critical if you expect an adequate income. You need to be self-directed and disciplined. Each day you must do work—making a client contact, developing a client, working on a project or on self-development. No day should be a vacation day!

Self-Management

If you are just beginning as a consultant, you should have an adequate income to carry you through the first year or two so you can survive on your own without counting on winning a big contract. If you don't have that kind of income, get yourself an adequate financial cushion. You can't be truly effective in your new business if you are constantly worried about money and making payments each month.

Consulting Cycle

The consulting cycle is simple to understand. You make a presentation to a potential client. You negotiate the fees and arrangements for payment. You perform the service, and you submit an invoice.

Consultant Tips

It takes the following skills and attributes to be a successful training consultant:

1. specific, valuable experience and expertise
2. ability to make sales calls and manage the sales process
3. good telephone skills
4. good people skills
5. good organizer of time
6. self-starter (every day)
7. ability to handle finances
8. flexibility
9. belief in self
10. contacts
11. comfort working alone
12. patience and respect for all points of view
13. ability to know when to seek advice and accept help

14. business and market sense

15. code of ethics.

Tips on Contracting

Here is a checklist of events and activities that you should review before you meet your client or conduct a personal survey activity (PSA) over the telephone:

1. *Client's needs:* Talk with the client to determine what he or she needs and wants. Also determine the following through discussions with the client or your own observations: the client or company norms, the mission of the organization, and the backgrounds of the perspective learners.

2. *Time constraints:* Determine the number of training days, typical training schedule, beginning and ending times, and lunch arrangements. Also discuss the spacing of training days and the pacing of material.

3. *Location:* Suggest that training take place at a neutral location away from the office and telephones. Prior to training, you should visit the site and look at the physical setup, equipment, and the "comfort" of the proposed meeting site. Also check the room layout to be sure it suits your needs.

4. *Trainees' roles and experience:* Determine the roles on the job and what previous training programs learners have attended.

5. *Trainers' roles:* Establish the trainer's role and responsibilities. Also be sure trainers have access to key stakeholders in the organization.

6. *Group size:* Determine the size of the group and decide the method you will use to create work groups and learning communities within the training event.

7. *Opportunity for follow-up:* Establish if there is a chance to meet with the learners and the organization to measure the return-on-investment of the training time and dollars.

You go through three stages during the contract meeting:

1. *Opening:* In your introduction, establish the need for the meeting. You might also want to develop an agenda for everyone to follow.

2. *Body:* In this stage, you present your findings and determine whether the client's interest or needs matches your portfolio of skills (and interests).

3. *Closing:* Summarize the important things that you provide the client. Make sure you have a "power close."

RESPONDING TO A TRAINING REQUEST   TIP #2

A major portion of your training design time will be devoted to requests that you receive from managers. Figure 2 shows the steps that the trainer or course designer goes through when investigating and responding to a training request.

GUIDE FOR DESIGNING TRAINING
PROGRAMS WITH A TEAM   TIP #3

When a training staff works together to design a program, it must achieve a high level of efficiency and creativity. If the staff members for a training program are new to one another, initial time (perhaps as much as an afternoon or an evening) should be scheduled for them to do their own team building. A much-needed tool is a guide for staff members that not only describes what should be done but also suggests the sequence to be followed.

The staff typically must take up the following considerations, in approximately the order given, as it prepares a training event. Here are 10 easy steps to guide the group through the process.

1. Evaluate the documented training need or needs.
   • What data do you have on the participants' jobs, home environment, age, gender, and level of skill?
   • What are the participants' expectations for the training program?
   • Has a proper questionnaire been administered?

Figure 2. Flow chart.

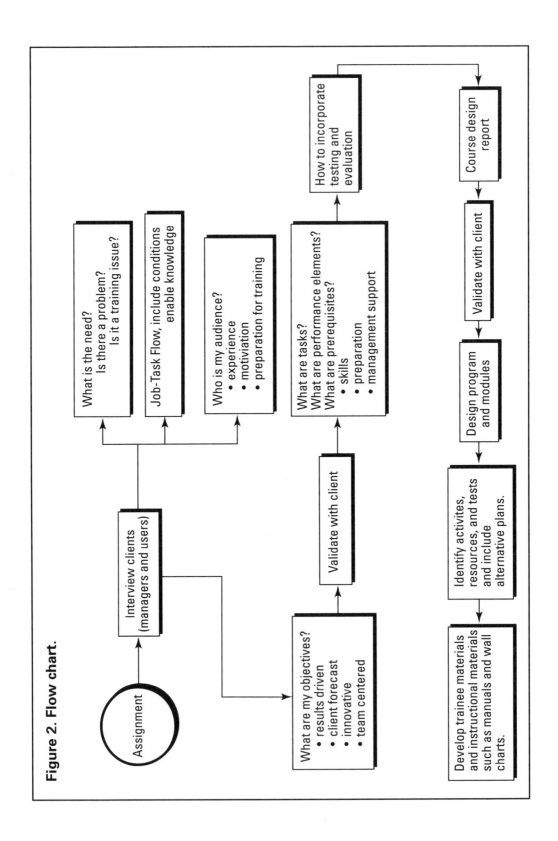

- Has the team seen the program announcement?
- What is known about the participants' motivation and readiness?
- What further information does the team need to obtain at the beginning of the program?

2. Set training goals.
   - Discuss and write a set of goals for the program, usually not more than five, and have them ready for use in the first session.
   - Agree among yourselves on the difference between goals and objectives.
   - Be explicit about values, the methods to be used, and any ground rules.
   - Establish trainer's responsibilities together with the design team.

3. Assess staff resources and skills.
   - What training aids and devices have staff members brought with them?
   - What special skills and interests exist among staff members?
   - If certain unusual modules are needed, who can handle them?
   - What recourses are required to develop the training response?

4. Select training strategies and prioritize the order for the program events.
   - This is the heart of the design: What should come first, second, and so forth?
   - Block out the time schedule on a flipchart and start filling it in.
   - Begin with known elements, such as meals, breaks, and beginning and ending times.
   - As other elements are filled in, look at the schedule's balance, flow, and required energy level.
   - Mornings are better for theory; afternoons are better for activity; evenings for nonverbal events.

One thing should lead to another. Will the experience of the participants be one of growth and development, or will it seem to them that they are getting a series of unconnected inputs?

5. State the objectives for each module of the program.
   - This may be done by the staff, through discussion, or by the staff members responsible for a specific module.
   - Ideally, the objectives should be specific and measurable: "By the end of this period you should be able to. . . ."
   - Present objectives to participants at the start of each session. Knowing where they are going will help them to learn better.

6. Predict the time schedule for each element of the modules.
   - Each element in the schedule should be specific: introduction, 10 minutes; forming groups and giving instructions, five minutes; working on the task, 40 minutes; and so forth.
   - On a larger scale, make sure that sufficient time is available for what is planned for each training element.
   - Make use of time. Consider how much time the training requires. If you don't have enough time, cover less. The participants will not learn anything if they are hurried through the learning process.

7. Allocate a staff member who will be responsible for each element.
   - Generally, all staff members participate in the first session. Planning this session often takes a large portion of the total planning time. At this meeting, it is best to establish the roles and responsibilities of the members and the expected level of participation. Send a follow-up memo recording the discussion and agreement of the roles and responsibilities the next day. Do not wait more than a week. Things change. People forget.
   - For subsequent modules, individual staff members or pairs volunteer to take responsibility.
   - All staff need not participate in planning every session.
   - No one should be overburdened or underutilized. This is a good time to establish a norm regarding when and how staff members can help one another. For example, they must decide whether it's okay for other staff to interrupt when a staff member is doing a presentation.

Schedule time for planning and checking sessions with the staff. Few programs run their course without alteration. When will the staff get together? Can it be done during working hours so that meetings will not consume all available free time or go on late at night?

8. Assess the logistical elements including:
    • space—large room, small room, comfort, convenience
    • materials—handouts, pencils, flipcharts, name tents, magic markers, videotape, reference materials
    • housekeeping details—breaks, meals, hotels, and so forth
    • administration—registration, money, travel, personal supplies
    • recreation—indoor-outdoor resources, alone time, and socializing time.

9. Define the primary clients' concerns.
    • Who is the primary client? Who is paying for this?
    • What are the client expectations? How will you communicate?
    • So far, does your design meet these expectations?
    • What contact will you have with the client before, during, and after the program?
    • Will the client be expected to take action as a result of the program?
    • Are you and the client clear on your contract?

10. Provide for an evaluation.
    • Will you evaluate in the following way as part of the design:
        — by obtaining postmeeting reaction sheets for each module?
        — by obtaining a daily rating of satisfaction or learning?
        — by obtaining an end-of-program evaluation?
    • Each of these needs preparation. Who is going to do it?
    • Is there any provision for follow-up?
    • Is there a requirement for a report to the primary client?
    • Do you anticipate that the design as planned will meet the goals stated?

COURSE OBJECTIVES   TIP #4

Course objectives should represent a clear statement of what participants should do after they've received the training. This information comes from your task analysis.

In practice, therefore, you will have at least twice as many statements as you have tasks on your list. These statements will have the following characteristics:

- An objective says something about the learners. It does not describe the resource materials, the trainer, or the type of learning activity.
- An objective describes the learners' behavior or performance. It does not describe the performance of the trainer or what the learners are expected to know or understand. If you use the verb *to understand,* you must go on to explain what learners are expected to do to demonstrate that understanding. Whatever it is you mean by *understanding* would be defined in the sentences to follow the general one.
- An objective is about outcomes. It describes an action and not the process that the learner went through to get there. The objective describes what the learner is expected to be like at the end of the training, rather than the process the learner used to get to the end.
- An objective describes the conditions under which learners will perform the terminal behavior. For example, a learner will answer three problems with the use of a slide rule or calculator. Remember, anything that the learner will use to perform the task must be defined in the objective statement.
- An instructional objective also includes information about the level of performance that will be considered acceptable. If a learner will be expected to perform a task within five minutes at the end of a module, this must be stated as part of the objective.

Following are three examples of objectives from Mager (1975):

1. Given an unfinished metal casting, be able to surface, drill, and tap according to the specifications indicated on the attached blueprint without error, in three of five demonstrations.
2. Provided with an outdoor television cable dish kit and appropriate tools, be able to install the dish correctly. Connect the input lead to the telephone line connection. Performance will

be judged correct if the dish installation is completed according to trade standards and if the selected cable channels function.

3. Performance: Be able to point out forest fire hazards in a forest area.

    Behavior: Identify dangerous conditions by pointing.

    Conditions: The learner must have access to forest areas and be exposed to dangerous conditions determined by the instructor.

    Criteria: Given a descriptive list of dangerous situations, rank order them according to most to least dangerous.

COURSE CONSTRUCTION   TIP #5

The most critical part of a training course happens before you enter the training room. Here's an overview of the essential design and development steps. In the course design phase, you plan the course. In the course development phase, you develop the materials and training activities.

Design Basics

A course design is a guide for developing the training scheme and the learning activities. You develop this scheme on the basis of the learning objectives that you wrote after you conducted the needs assessment process.

The course design plan should specify funding categories, such as personnel, equipment and supplies, and facilities. Additionally, consider the total budget for the training. Define the scope of the course and develop a project plan that specifies people's roles and responsibilities and deadlines for course development.

The final equipment and supply list will emerge only after the lesson plans have been completed, but an estimate of the costs should be included.

Underlying Course Objective

The first step in the course design phase is to determine the training course objective. The course objective states the purpose or benefits of the course, learning objectives state what the learner should know or be able to do after the course, and enabling objectives describe the steps that the learner needs to master to achieve the learning objective.

Definitive Course Description

Writing a statement of the course objective is like putting a word puzzle together. Some words you know, others you don't. Here's a list of the information you should include in your description:

- why the course is needed, including course objectives, expected benefits, and value of the benefits
- who is involved, including the intended trainees, subject-matter experts, supervisors, consultants, and suppliers, as well as their availability for the project
- what the course will cover, including general course content, skill and knowledge areas to be improved, an explanation of how the skill and knowledge areas have been identified and analyzed, and descriptions of how learners will demonstrate the new skill or knowledge, or both
- how the content will be arranged in sequence and what strategies will be used to engage learners in the learning process
- how much the training course is expected to cost and how it will be funded as well as any areas in which cost savings may be realized.

Setting the Course and Module Design

During the analysis phase, you identify whether certain tasks or routines are subordinate to others that must be performed in a certain sequence or are unrelated to them. Therefore, you must design the order in which the information will be presented. To maximize the learning, you'll develop a scheme to present this content. Here are a few suggested strategies:

- hierarchical, in which learners receive an overview of the course content before moving to specific elements
- sequential, in which learners are taught steps that lead to a given conclusion

- job order, in which learners are taught tasks as they would occur on the job
- priority order, in which the skill or knowledge areas that are essential to task completion are taught first
- topical order, in which instruction is knowledge-based but not sequential, such as the benefits of a new product.

Selecting the Instructional Strategy

You should choose a strategy for each of the learning objectives. The strategy should include the enabling objective and an outline of course content, media, expected feedback mechanism, and level of evaluation and method. The time that you invest in planning this stage will ease the development process.

When making decisions about which media are most appropriate to convey the message, assess the costs in a variety of ways to determine which option best suits the investment you're willing to make. Consider, for example:

- whether you'll have to spend a significant amount of money to buy, rent, or purchase a product
- whether you'll have to spend a significant amount of time to locate, create, or develop a product
- whether you'll need assistance from outside the training department, such as from vendors.

Once you've made these decisions, you are ready to move to the development phase.

Developing the Course

During the development phase, media and materials will be located, selected, or created. Among the items that need to be gathered, created, or designed are the following:

- instructional guides, such as lesson plans, bridges that lead from one instructional activity to the next
- integrators that serve to tie activities together and align them with the learner's prior learning

- administrative aids, such as participant rosters, maps, checklists for materials and equipment, and name tags for learners
- learner guides, such as text, workbooks, and job aids
- evaluation materials
- activity aids, such as checklists, role-play scripts, case studies, and laboratory exercises
- equipment and supplies, paper, videotapes, VCRs, films, wall charts, computers, flipcharts, markers and spare equipment parts.

Evaluation Materials

An evaluation may be formative or summative, but it must be tied to the course and the learning objectives. A formative evaluation continues throughout the analysis, design, development, and implementation phases of instructional development. A formative evaluation plan describes the means for improving a course and for assessing learners' training progress and attitudes toward the training. A summative evaluation occurs after course completion. A summative evaluation plan describes such measures as posttraining performance, turnover, and customer comments.

By answering questions about tasks, topics, learning activities, materials, tests, and productivity, evaluations can lead to course refinements. Evaluations can be conducted at the objective's level through tests of learners' mastery of the enabling objectives or the learning objectives. Evaluations also may be conducted by use of group-related and enabling objectives. The trainer executes this method by asking each group of learners to write one question on any topic or issue that he or she feels needs to be clarified. The trainer can either answer questions posed by each group or rotate each set of questions and have each group of learners answer a neighboring group's question. After completing this step, the trainer should take note of anything that seems to be a design course or material development issue and share it with the course designer. It could be that material needs to be added or deleted to ensure that the evaluation adequately tests the learner against the standards for the targeted objective.

Anchoring Administration

Course administration ties all of the course elements—the enabling, learning, and course objectives. This is the last step before the course presentation. At this stage you add bridges, special learning activities, and variety.

Among the items to be considered are the following:

- *Activity sequence:* What were the learners doing immediately before the presentation of the objective? What will they be doing immediately after? What relationship exists between the previous and subsequent activities? Are the learners aware of the relationship? Is there a logical transition from one activity to the next?

- *Directions:* What instructions will the trainer need in order to convey the information or content? How specific should they be? What instructions do the learners need in order to complete any participatory activities? How will tests be conducted?

- *Materials:* What visual aids or handouts are needed? Are they in order and ready when required? Are all supplies available? Are props such as models or reference books handy?

- *Hardware:* What kinds of equipment—models, videotape players, flipcharts, computers, and so forth—are required by the content? Are they in good working order? Are spare parts or alternative methods available in the event of equipment failure?

- *Special environments:* If a training program requires a special environment, like a computer lab, is that environment available?

- *Class management:* What are the requirements for conducting the course, for example, the optimal number of learners? What seating arrangements are required? Is special access needed for any handicapped learner? Will lunch or coffee be served? How will this service be handled?

- *Required records:* The course design document will detail what course records will be kept, how, by whom, and for how long. Training records may be kept on paper, computer disks, zip drives, or CDs. Original or back-up records may be maintained in the training information system or the planning or legal departments.

Original training records or copies may need to be forwarded to a government agency, private regulatory group, or professional agency that issues credentials. Record retention and destruction schedules may be established by law, organizational policies, or by the design team's recommendation.

During development, any documentation materials could be copied. For example, the training department probably has a standard daily attendance form that needs only to be copied. But a new legally mandated course might require a form that documents employees' attendance in specific units of a course.

An organization will typically keep a history that shows responsibility for various aspects of course development; form samples, the course design document, and lesson plans; budgets; attendance by learners, trainers, facilitators, and guests; and evaluation records about individual participants, the instructor's performance, and course effectiveness or efficiency.

- *Standards of performance:* Training designs should be performance-based, that is, that the training should focus on mastery of skills that can be immediately transferred back on the job.

The standards of successful job performance must be clear to the learners by the trainers, and success in training should be measured by the successful transfer of learning. Successful training programs are designed around what the learners need to know and how to transfer the learning into on-the-job performance.

DIFFICULT SITUATIONS   TIP #6

Every training session is different, as you will discover, and every learner is different. Following is a list of the most frequently occurring difficult situations along with suggested ways to resolve them.

- *The group remains silent.* There are times when groups are silent, and that's fine. Other times, when groups should be interactive and engaging, they look at you with dead stares and keep silent. This is a scary situation for the trainer. One of the things that you can do is check it out. Ask the group if there is a reason for their silence. It could be that they don't understand what you are presenting, that your method of delivery makes them uncomfortable, or that your method of delivery is one they're not familiar with.

- *Things are moving too quickly.* Sometimes the group picks up something that you have said that relates to material that you'll cover later. You can respond simply and state when you are going to cover it, or if shifting the piece of information or module makes sense, you can insert it during the present discussion. Not all learners are comfortable with taking things out of the design sequence, however, so you might request a show of hands on whether to change the order.

- *Things are moving too slowly.* The group may not be motivated to listen to your topic, or it may have expected you to present something other than what you are presenting. If this occurs during training, try to build on things the participants already know if it seems to you that the information is too basic; don't speed up your presentation, but encourage trainees to participate. Situations like this are good times to develop an in-class game, conduct a competitive team answer quiz, or find another way to enliven the lesson.

- *A talkative learner is in the group.* This is fine unless the person seems to dominate every conversation. One suggestion is that you enlist that person's help as an expert. Another idea is to talk with the person during the break, acknowledging his or her expertise and suggesting you work together so that everyone has an opportunity to participate.

- *A silent learner, one who does not ask questions, is in the group.* Don't jump to conclusions about silent learners. Although it appears that they're not listening or participating, they might be auditory learners, who listen, process, and only ask questions or make comments when it is essential for to clarify something that is confusing. If one is in the group, first check out the person's learning style to determine how he or she learns best. If you find the situation is not one of learning style, try and bring the person into the group. Assign the person to a caring participant or group. Tread cautiously. Start with asking fairly easy questions or ask the person to share an experience. If all else fails, during the break you might ask the person in a private conversation how the training is going for him or her. Find out if there is anything that the person might need.

- *A typical know-it-all is in the group.* The know-it-all corrects everyone constantly, sometimes you. Don't kill the person on sight. Find out what's going on. Or as happens in most group situations, the group will sort this problem out for you.

- *A session is getting sidetracked.* Sometimes a conversation starts in the right direction but finishes up in the wrong place. Acknowledge this and get the group back on track. You might want to have a person in the group monitor those side trips. Have someone in each group be a parking lot attendant by recording issues that need attention and placing them in the parking lot until you can address them.

- *The trainer and a learner have personality problems.* Occasionally you'll have a personality clash with one of the participants. The professional trainer must ignore this and continue treating that participant in a normal manner. Avoid letting the group see the problem.

- *Participants have a personality problem.* Personality problems do occur in the classroom environment because people don't leave their personality at the door. If arguments start between participants, you must cut in quickly. Ask others for comments on the issue. Try to keep the personalities separated. If the situation is not resolved, during the break, have a frank discussion with both parties.

- *A rambler is in the group.* Some people learn by speaking. A rambling participant could be this person. Practice good active listening techniques. Ask the rambler for the bottom-line message so that the whole group might participate. Be patient. Be polite yet firm in bring the discussion to a close.

- *An arguer is in the group.* This person might also have to be put in the trainer's blind spot. Most of the time, the group will take care of this type. Use your judgment. You could suggest that the discussion continue after class or that the class devote some time for the specific issue during a lunch discussion.

- *A complainer is in the group.* If the complaint is not something that must be addressed, you could explore the issue briefly, but don't waste the group's time on it. If you get complaints about the organization, let the participants know this is not the correct forum in which to discuss a change of policy.

- *Side conversations take place during training.* Although I've seen some trainers ask people who talk during training to share their conversation, I don't suggest this at all. Instead, change their seats or talk to the people. But don't gang up on them. In this kind of situation, the group will always support other learners, no matter how badly they've behaved. Polite, nonthreatening action is the way to handle this situation.

- *A learner gives a definitely wrong response.* Don't embarrass the person by saying the answer is wrong. You could acknowledge the person's point of view and suggest that he or she consider some additional data. Or you could use the correct information in a summary of the person's response. Some trainers suggest asking the participants for their comments, but be careful with this strategy. Participants may embarrass one another or become contentious, and you may not have the power to resolve the dispute.

TYPES OF TRAINING   TIP #7

Training Formats

There are two types of training strategies: learner-centered and trainer-centered. In learner-centered training, learners control the learning process. They set the pace and the amount of material to be covered. In learner-centered training, the trainer and learner typically have two-way communication and a collaborative dialogue. Distance learning courses are learner centered.

In trainer-centered learning, the trainer establishes the format, the content, and the timing. Lectures are trainer centered. Communication is one way, and the trainer controls the dialogue.

Following are descriptions of the most common training formats:

- *Classroom:* This is a traditional approach to training. In most cases, this is structured seating, usually in rows, a given agenda, and little active movement. The classroom style is conducive to lectures.

- *Outdoor adventures:* This learner-centered format is sometimes referred to an adventure learning event. The military has used this format for years. Over the past 10 years, this method has been used for building team training and leadership development. To be effective, it must be linked to meaningful classroom input and an extensive debriefing session. Also, make sure you look into the insurance liability issue before you decide to develop your program using this method.

- *Computer assisted:* Sometimes called computer-based training (CBT) or programmed learning, this learner-centered method teaches people material at computer workstations in a programmed way; the lessons in the programmed learning are usually designed and developed as action-based tasks or in other words, step-by-steps. With the spread of computers and telecourses, this process provides flexibility so that learners can control their pace. The disadvantage is that learners are most often alone during the learning sessions. If you are thinking about using this method, conduct a thorough cost analysis to determine the need and the magnitude of the use and the stability of the information (avoid constant updates) before making the investment.

- *Training media:* These media include overhead projectors and flipcharts, which are used in trainer-centered formats, videotapes, and liquid crystal displays (LCDs), which can be used in either learner- or trainer-centered formats. When using instructional media, aim for a variety in both method and media to break up the learners' experience and enable the training message to get through on different levels.

Training Roles

Trainers have to wear different hats. In some companies, a trainer will be able to share responsibilities with other people in the training department, but in other companies one person may have several roles. A subject matter expert will be able to assist a trainer in areas where the trainer does not have expertise.

- *Trainer:* The role of the trainer is to facilitate learning so that learners can acquire the key competencies presented. A trainer should be good at presenting information so that the attention of the audience is held and the information is accurately conveyed.

— *Method expert:* As a trainer, you must exercise sound, professional judgment about the best process to use in presenting and facilitating learning. Becoming competent with a variety of learning techniques should be your constant goal and part of your professional development plan. Watch other trainers, attend training events, read about training, share ideas with other trainers. Take risks by trying different training methods and experimenting.

— *Group manager:* The role of the group manager takes a while to acquire. Subject competency can be acquired fairly quickly, but group facilitation skills take much longer. A good and experienced facilitator has a skill of enormous power and is able to harness the synergy within the group to achieve powerful and lasting learning. It is a competency you should strive to acquire and is best acquired through practice.

• *Subject expert:* The subject matter expert (SME) knows the content and task well and is responsible for providing information about them. Whereas the trainer is responsible for designing and developing the content and process so that trainees comprehend and use the information provided, the SME is the quality control person who ensures the accuracy of the training. The SME is your partner in designing and delivering training.

GAMES, SIMULATIONS, AND ROLE PLAYS   TIP #8

Through games, simulations, and role plays, learners can discover learning outcomes on their own, without being told everything. The ultimate outcome for using games, simulations, and role plays is to improve learning.

• *Games:* A game is an activity, illustration, or exercise that can support the point the trainer presents. Typically, games are brief nonthreatening learning events in which all learners participate. They should have simple, uncomplicated directions and a stated purpose that is consistent with the key competencies being taught, and, in most cases, they should be fun.

- *Simulations:* Sometimes referred to as case studies in action, simulations are highly participative training that is used mainly to teach skills and is linked to real-world situations. Simulations can be simple paper mock-ups or an exact replica of something like a tractor or nuclear reactor. Flight simulations in which pilots learn flying skills and procedures for dealing with emergency situations, for example, are realistic imitations of the real world. Another example is an in-box exercise for managers or office producers in which an entire office process is replicated with assigned roles, dialogues, and feedback mechanisms.

- *Role plays:* A role play is similar to a simulation. Normally the only prop needed for the role play is a script or short case study or problem, which the learners will act out. The problem is usually related to a situation at work that involves the players. After the role players have identified the problem, they act out the parts either as they would normally or by trying new behaviors. Following the role play, the players, often as well as other group members, provide feedback by identifying good and bad points, suggesting other forms of behavior, and recommending other alternatives. In a training situation, use this method of instruction selectively. Carefully judge the appropriate time for it and application of it because learners get bored with the format. Vary it by using other peripherals or methods.

TUTORIALS—INDIVIDUALIZED INSTRUCTION   TIP #9

Successful individualized instruction requires the completion of four major phases. Each phase is equally important and should be completed in sequence to ensure that you obtain the expected results from the training event. Omission of any of these phases can seriously affect the effectiveness of the tutorial program. The four major phases are preparation, presentation, performance, and follow-up. Following are descriptions of each:

1. *Preparation:* Ask the learner to define the problem or areas of need; have that person do the necessary analysis to ensure that there is a focused training need. Take the defined need or needs and develop a list of targeted training topics. Check this list with the learner.

Once you have a list of targeted topics, ask the learner to do a job breakdown. Learners must identify with their specific need for training before they can comprehend the why's and what's of their job. You can use the job breakdown to establish the design of your training course and to cluster your proposed training topics.

2. *Presentation:* Once you have provided the initial rationale as to why the topics are sequenced and how each piece of information you are to present is aligned, you are ready to begin the tutorial. The tutorial consists of the following three steps:

Step one: First, show and tell how it is done.

Step two: The second time through, demonstrate while asking the learner to explain why it's being done the way it is.

Step three: The third time, tell the learner what to do and have the learner do each step while explaining how and why it should be done that way. If at any point the learner provides incorrect information while explaining, coach the person until he or she has the correct information.

3. *Performance:* During the performance phase, the learner tries to perform each step of the assigned task. Again, the performance phase is frequently repeated several times so that the learner has a chance to check for understanding.

One way to accomplish this task is to ask the learner to explain what he or she is going to do, how he or she will do it, and why. Here you are checking to determine if the learner mastered the concepts you just presented. You check for understanding of both the content and the process. It may appear that the learner has mastered the content concepts but has interpreted the process differently. If the difference is a result of the person's own learning style, there is no problem. If the process is muddled, however, it usually means that the person has muddled the process conceptually and not learned the parts well.

By using this repetition in both the presentation and performance phases of the training sequence, the learner goes through the process at least five times. By this time, the learner has the key learning points mastered.

4. *Follow-Up:* The follow-up phase can be crucial to maintaining the mastery of the newly learned concepts. Once the learner performs adequately, check occasionally to make sure the person is using the proper methods.

This step is going to be difficult for you to administer unless you give the learner a posttutorial assignment and reach some agreement prior to departure as to how you both are going to manage this process.

Preparing for Tutorial Instruction

To prepare to conduct a tutorial, you have to know both the nature of the training need and the nature of the skills or knowledge that you'll be presenting to the learner. So in this first step, you'll have to collect and review all the necessary data (topical information) and organize it. Following is a self-preparation checklist:

- Describe and define the nature of the training situation.
- Analyze the situation and make sure that tutorial training is appropriate.
- Review the worksheets that you used to map out your training proposal. Make sure that you state a theoretical concept in your proposed design and development strategy.
- If you haven't done so already, prepare training objectives for the training you plan to do. Decide, in advance, where you're going and what you plan to accomplish in the training event.
- Prepare a job task breakdown sheet for each task that will be taught.
- Prepare a learning outline.
- Schedule an appropriate time and place for the training.
- Assemble any training aids or materials that you will need for the training. Assemble all materials and supplies, set up the equipment, and make other final preparations for the training.

When you've gotten yourself ready and the materials and the training site set up, and the learner has shown up for the tutorial, it's time to prepare the learner.

Preparing the Learner

Trainers often overlook this step, but it is very important in getting the learner in the right frame of mind to enter the training process. This is where you, the trainer, begin to apply the ARAB effectiveness key: *A* = Arouse, *R* = Reward, *A* = Assess, *B* = Build.

You *A*rouse the learners' curiosity and obtain an interest in the training; you *B*uild or maintain the learner's motivation. And although *R*eward and reinforcement will probably have to wait until the learners actually try out the newly learned concepts back on the job, you still *A*ssess the learning transfer before they go back in the workplace and make the appropriate learning links for the learners before they leave.

Presenting the Training

Now that you're ready to do the training, and the learners have been motivated to view the coming training in a favorable light (by using the ARAB method), you're ready to explain the actual steps of the tutorial.

This could be referred to as the show-and-tell step of the training. You'll be showing the steps of the course, telling how to perform them, and explaining why the training (and the related job) is done the way it is.

CONTRACT LEARNING   TIP # 10

Contract learning is a form of self-directed learning. Contract learning lets learners decide the topics or competencies they want to learn and how they want to learn them. Each learner can devise the topics to be mastered or the issues to be researched. This type of learning has a lot of advantages over the classroom style in which learners may just sit and listen to a lecture or become minimally involved in it.

In contract learning, trainers and learners prepare the contract. Learners also have the opportunity to write their own objectives, to determine what work is going to be done and what resources are going to be used, and to design the evaluation criteria. Because learners write so much, they really own the project. This sense of ownership gives them the motivation to carry the project or contract through to the finish.

The Learning Contract

The learning contract is a written agreement of the learner and the advisor or facilitator. In it, the learner and the trainer or facilitator establish that one or more competencies need to be raised to a higher level of expertise. Given this need statement, the learner enters into a formal, written agreement with the trainer or facilitator.

Once the two parties agree on the basic learning competencies, the learner and facilitator must agree on the learning objectives, resources, proof of goals met, and the evaluation process. Contract learning may be a totally learner-based process that the learner conducts without a trainer or facilitator. That approach might be problematic because no one would be able to check the administration of it and keep the learner on track. If the learner were unable to establish a workable contract, he or she could become discouraged and sidetracked from learning.

The typical contract has nine steps, as figure 3 shows. Through their negotiations, however, learners and trainers may choose more or fewer

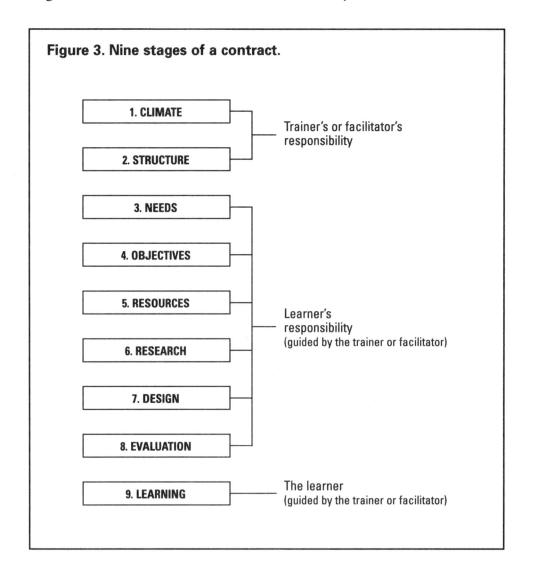

Figure 3. Nine stages of a contract.

1. CLIMATE

2. STRUCTURE

Trainer's or facilitator's responsibility

3. NEEDS

4. OBJECTIVES

5. RESOURCES

6. RESEARCH

Learner's responsibility (guided by the trainer or facilitator)

7. DESIGN

8. EVALUATION

9. LEARNING

The learner (guided by the trainer or facilitator)

steps as they reach terms acceptable to the learner. The key points for adult learners are that the contract contain a structure, objectives, evaluation method, and targeted learning outcomes.

Contract Elements

A number of styles are possible for learner contracts, but the most popular is a letter format. The elements for the letter come from a form like that in figure 4.

Before the learner and trainer can formulate a contract, they must identify the level of competency, which goes in the competency line in the figure. Then they can develop one or more specific learning objectives. These statements, which they list in the first column in the figure, must define what the learner will learn, not what that person will be doing.

Then the learner must establish the process for monitoring the contract, the resources needed, and the learning strategies required for meeting the objectives. These could include meeting or speaking with a subject matter expert, watching videotapes, reading specific literature, or working in a specific situation, whether real or simulated. These items would be entered in the second column.

In the third column, the learner must define the process for evaluating the learning. This section of the contract should contain specific statements as to products or actions that provide evidence of mastery. Examples might include essays, reports, projects, problem-solving situations, videotaped presentations, rating scales, or anything else that the evaluator can use to establish evidence of task accomplishment.

In the fourth section, the learner provides the measurement criteria. The learner could specify the length of an end-of-project report, standards for videotapes, required content and format for reports and the review process, criteria for evaluations, and comments or feedback.

When the learner has completed these four elements, both parties will review the contract and then sign it. The following checklist can help the parties decide if the contract is a sound document:

- Are the learning objectives specific?
- Do the objectives relate to the learning task?
- Are the resources and strategies appropriate to achieve the outcome?

Figure 4. Elements of a learning contract.

STUDENT _____ COMPETENCY _____ DATE

COMMENCED __/__/__

TRAINER OR FACILITATOR _____ DATE DUE __/__/__

1. Learning objectives	2. Resource strategies	3. What is to be assessed?	4. How is it to be assessed?
Write all of the learning objectives here. The learner should design more than one objective. The objectives must be easy to understand and must describe the learning, not the doing.	List all resources and strategies here. Include not only books and films but also human resources. There also may be a number of other items that need to be carried out by the learner: they also should be included here.	The things that are being assessed should relate directly to the stated learning objectives. However, here we are normally looking at what has been done. This could include reports, essays, videotapes, diary details, or situations.	Assessment could state the length of the report or essay. It could include a time frame for a video presentation. It also could state that certain experts must agree with the results and the process by which they were achieved. Did the trainer or facilitator think the resources were used effectively?

(Please note that these are only suggestions. Anything can be included as long as both the learner and the trainer or facilitator agree to its relevance and appropriateness.)

Approved: Yes ☐   Advisor's signature: _____

No ☐

Date: __/__/__   Learner's signature: _____

- Are there any additional resources required?
- Are the items being assessed appropriate for the learning situation?

- Can the learner think of any other form of evaluation?
- Are the evaluation criteria fair?
- Has the grading or evaluation process been established?
- Have the steps for completing and presenting the contract learning been defined?

Conclusion

Contract learning can be developed for any learning situation; it is a learning process. It can be of value to both learners and trainers or facilitators because there are benefits to both in managing the process. The benefit for the trainer in this process is facilitating the learning process and helping learners achieve their goals.

In designing this self-directed learning process, the trainer or facilitator must create a process that involves learners' participation from the initial stage. This involvement serves two purposes. One, it sets the scene for learners to design what they want to learn, the format for the learning and the outcome, and two, it allows learners to take maximum responsibility for the learning process.

Learning contracts help to solve problems associated with the differences in educational backgrounds, life experiences, personal interests, job experiences, different forms of motivation, and general abilities of the individuals.

RETENTION EXERCISES   TIP #11

Michele Mattia of the American Management Association developed a dozen proven review techniques.

To ensure learners retain what they've learned, Mattia says follow these guiding points:

- Identify what the learner has learned, not what the trainer has trained. Tests are a judge only of what you, the trainer, have provided. They don't measure what's important to the learner.
- For maximum retention, vary the ways to learn what you are training, and review the content at least six times during the training day.
- Involve the learners. People remember things that are different, colorful, and graphic.

- Create handouts so trainees have something concrete to take with them when they leave. These are far more effective than oral summaries.

Technique #1: What Did You Learn?

What You Need	How To Do It
6 blank flip sheets and markers	• Each person visits each sheet twice to record a learning point from the day's training. • Each point is unique (no repeats). • Divide large groups into small groups and have them update lists. • Check any item the learner does not understand. The person who wrote it must explain it.

Technique #2: One Blooming Point!

What You Need	How To Do It
• An inflated, different-colored balloon for each table • Small Post-It notes	• Each balloon has a label relevant to a single topic covered. • Each member of the table writes one idea about the topic on a Post-It and attaches it to the balloon. • The balloon with the notes remains at the table for duration of the session. As participants remember ideas, they can add Post-Its.

Technique #3: Collect the dots

What You Need	How To Do It
• Colored dots • Markers • Flipchart sheets—one for each table or group. Each sheet should list specific topics under discussion.	• Each morning provide different colored dots. Each person gets a different colored dot. • Each person marks with a dot anything useful or relevant to his or her work that is on the flipchart. • At day's end, participants identify their dots on the flipchart sheet.

Technique #4: Three Important Things

What You Need	How To Do It
• Flipchart paper • Markers	• Give this take-away assignment at day's end: identify three important things you learned today. • Next morning each participant will list the three on a flipchart. • Keep each sheet posted on wall.

Technique #5: Surprise Catch

What You Need	How To Do It
• Koosh balls	• Participants stand. Instructor models behavior: "I choose [the name of a participant]," and throws the ball. The person who catches must call out a learning point from the day before.
	• The catcher then becomes the pitcher and throws the ball to another participant. Once ball is tossed, that pitcher sits down.

Technique #6: True-False Questions

What You Need	How To Do It
• 3 x 5 cards	• Have each group construct true-or-false questions (the number will depend on time) based on previous day's learning.
	• Teams compete answering them. When a team answers incorrectly, it sits down. The last team standing wins.

Technique #7: Jeopardy

What You Need	How To Do It
• 3 x 5 cards	• Have each table write a content question, one to a card (the number will depend on time). Collect them. • Line up the entire group, dividing them into two groups against two walls, spelling bee fashion. • Rotate asking questions to the first person in line on one side, and then to the other side. If the answer is wrong, the person sits down. • Keep going until one team eliminates the other.

Technique #8: Concept Puzzles

What You Need	How To Do It
• Colored cardboard (six to eight colors)	• Cut out simple puzzle pieces from each sheet of cardboard and list one concept per puzzle piece. Have each person take a piece. • Put the people holding all like-colored pieces together at the same table. • The group puts the puzzle together and lists six to eight learning points about the topics on each puzzle piece. • (You can cover a lot of ground with this review because it's so thorough.)

Technique #9: Card Game

What You Need	How To Do It
• 3 x 5 cards	• One card for each participant who writes one question about the content on it.
	• Collect the cards, shuffle, and deal equally to each table.
	• Give participants 15 minutes to answer the questions, using all resources available.
	• Participants list the answers on a flipchart.
	• Do a Q&A as a total group.

Technique #10: The Most Useful

What You Need	How To Do It
• Post-It dots	• Headline each sheet "The Most Useful Thing I Learned" (from previous session).
• Flipchart paper	• Each table lists the most useful things it comes up with, leaving $1/3$ of the page between statements.
• Markers	• Other participants move from chart to chart dotting with their initials each statement, and must try to "piggyback" an idea onto each statement. (Make sure that each participant lists a related idea under each statement he or she initials.)

Technique #11: Correct the Errors

What You Need	How To Do It
• Overhead • Transparencies • Green pens	• Create overheads with errors of content in them, not typographic errors. • Each participant should discover what the error is, write it down, and provide the right answer. • Each group compares the list of errors found and corrections. • Debrief the entire group.

Technique #12: Developing a Picture

What You Need	How To Do It
• Flipchart paper • Markers	• Assign each table a portion of the topic or the whole topic, if appropriate. • Tell the participants that there will be a visitor first thing in the morning who knows NOTHING about the topic. • Each table is to present the highlights of the topic in whatever fashion they wish. • Invite one or two guests to listen to the presentations. Ideally guests should be stakeholders in the training.

A skill is set of steps. Some examples of skills include word processing, driving, scuba diving, and flying a plane. Some skills require simple actions such as turning on an overhead projector. Other skills are more complex, like using the LCD for projection.

All skills require the use of three types of skills: motor, perceptual, and cognitive. A demonstration, generally, requires a combination of skills. This combination of motor, perceptual, and cognitive skills is given the term *psychomotor skill*. Therefore, regardless of the type of skill that you may be demonstrating, you must be mindful that all three skill areas are involved in the process.

The demonstration process consists of four sections: preparation, demonstration, practice, and assessment. Following is a detailed description of each section.

Preparation

The following steps in the process are an overview of the steps to help you prepare for the training event and present a professional learning event:

- Establish the current level of trainee knowledge or ability, or both, in the area to be presented.
- Discuss the skill to be presented with other SMEs, analyze the skill, and break it down into manageable teachable parts.
- Draft a plan for conducting the demonstration.
- Prepare the support materials for the training event, job aids, wall charts, videotapes, and so forth.
- Prepare lesson objectives and test items.
- Prepare an introduction to the training event that is appropriate to the situation.

Demonstration

It's important that you do the demonstration correctly—no flaws because you're modeling the way. There are a number of suggested ways to present a demonstration. The following method has seven steps.

1. *Demonstrate at normal speed:* Demonstrate the skill correctly, at normal speed, so that trainees can see the final result and can also see what is expected from them at the conclusion of the training.

2. *Demonstrate again slowly:* Demonstrate again for the trainees, this time doing it slowly so that they can see exactly what is being done. As the trainer demonstrates, trainees should begin to recognize names, parts, tools, and any obvious skills. When demonstrating and explaining how the skill is performed, trainers must be careful about what they say and how they say it. The trainer should introduce each step, then highlight the key points with deliberate and possibly exaggerated movements. These key points can also be highlighted by voice, by giving reasons, or perhaps by repetition. It's a good idea to pause between key points to let them sink in. The demonstrator must have a set of notes or a skill sheet to follow for this part of the demonstration. The skill sheet gives a complete breakdown of the skill, with the keypoints highlighted, and any tricks of the trade and safety points noted, as figure 5 shows.

3. *Verbal instruction from the trainees:* Next, get the trainees to tell you how to carry out the task in the correct sequence. The demonstrator carries out the performance as instructed by the trainees.

Practice

4. *Controlled trainee performance:* Have the trainees carry out the skill under close supervision and at a controlled pace. It is important that the trainees perform this exercise correctly. It is difficult, and sometimes also impossible, to counteract the effects of a skill learned incorrectly.

5. *Student practice:* Now is the time for students to practice. This part of a skill session should be at least 50 percent of the allocated session time. During this time, the demonstrator must be available to answer any questions that arise. Don't take over for trainees who have problems, but have them correct the problem

Figure 5. A sample skill sheet.

OPERATIONS	KEY POINTS	SAFETY
ASSEMBLE		
Position tank	• stand tank up • O-ring facing away	• Don't leave tank standing unattended
Position BCD	• Slide over tank • BCD facing away • Height of BCD should be ½ way up tank valve • Adjust to fit different size tanks (63 & 88) • Lock in position	• Avoid hitting head on tank valve • Must be secure so it doesn't fall out when straps are set
Position and attach regulator	• Remove dust cap • Regulator and octopus to right side • Machined face to O-ring • Do up finger tight • Connect low pressure inflator to DCD	• Keep out sand • Check O-ring is there • If too tight cannot undo later • Pull knurled nut back
Turn on air	•Turn tank on • Check tank pressure • Check 2nd stage regulator • Check octopus • Check L.P. inflator	• Slowly check position of gauges On and back ½ turn. What to do if O-ring missing • Must be full to commence dive • Must breath easily • Must inflate and deflate
Lay down	• Gauges and regula-tors in front	• Keep out sand and grass
DISMANTLE		
To turn off	• Turn air off • Purge lines	• Not over tight
Remove regulator	• Disconnect L.P. inflator • Undo nut • Replace dust cap • Place regulator away	• Must be dry

(Figure 5 *continued*)		
Remove BCD	• Undo Velcro • Slide off tank • Place BCD away	• Hold tank
Tank	• Lay tank down	• So it won't fall
FINAL		
Rinse all equipment		• Don't push purge button

themselves. The trainer or other members of the group can provide the correct information or suggestions. Try also to enlist their peers to assist with any problems.

Assessment

6. *Student assessment:* Some form of assessment must take place to ensure that the trainees have reached the stated objectives and standards that were described at the beginning of the session. Assessment may be done during the session by asking questions, or it may be done at the end of the session by using some form of test (written, practical, or other). The type of assessment generally depends on the demonstrator and the type of skill being instructed. An important point with assessment is that trainees should be expecting the type of test you give. The test also must be appropriate to the topic and the learning event.

7. *Conclusion:* The session must conclude with the demonstrator summarizing the main points of the session and clarifying any areas of concern. If possible, all test results should be made available before the end of the session, so they might be included in the conclusion.

References

Boyatzis, R.E. (1982). *The Competent Manager.* New York: John Wiley.

Broad, M., and Newstrom, J. (1992). *Transfer of Training.* Reading, MA: Addison-Wesley.

Caffarella, R. (1988). *Program Development and Evaluation Resource Book for Trainers,* Greeley, CO.

Hannum, W., and Hansen, C. (1989). *Instructional Systems Development in Large Organizations.* Englewood Cliffs, NJ: Educational Technology Publications.

Kirkpatrick, D. (1987). *Techniques for Evaluating Training Programs. More Evaluating Training Programs.* Alexandria, VA: American Society for Training & Development.

Kirkpatrick, D.L. (1994). *Evaluating Training Programs: The Four Levels.* San Francisco: Berrett-Koehler.

Kroehnert, G. (1994). *Basic Training for Trainers* (revised edition), 60–61. Australia: McGraw-Hill Book Company.

Laird, D. (1985). *Approaches to Training and Development.* Reading, MA: Addison-Wesley.

Mager, R. (1975). *Preparing Instructional Objectives* (2d edition). Belmont, CA: Fearon.

Marshall, V., and Schriver, R. (1994, January). Using Evaluation to Improve Performance. *Technical & Skills Training,* 6–9.

McArdle, G.E.H. (1998). *Conducting a Needs Assessment.* Menlo Park, CA: Crisp Publications.

Phillips, J.J. (1991). *Handbook of Training Evaluation and Measurement Methods.* Houston: Gulf.

Phillips, J.J. (1994). *Evaluating Training Programs: The Four Levels.* San Francisco: Berrett-Koehler.

Schuler, R.S. (1996). *Human Resource Management* (5th edition). Exhibit 9.8, Learning Principles to Increase the Effectiveness of Training, page 327. Cincinnati, OH: South Western College Publishing.

Silberman, M. (1990).

Society for Human Resource Management. (1997). *Society for Human Resource Management Learning System Certification Guide.* Alexandria, VA: Society for Human Resource Management.

Steadman, S.V. (1980, January). Learning to Select a Needs Assessment Strategy. *Training and Development Journal,* 56–61.

Suggested Reading

CHAPTER 2

Barney, Jay B., and Patrick M. Wright. (1998, Spring). "On Becoming a Strategic Partner: The Role of Human Resources in Gaining Competitive Advantage." *Human Resource Management, 37*(1), 31–46.

Caudron, Shari. (1998, May). "Integrate HR and Training." *Workforce, 77*(5), 88–93.

Dell, Jay, John Fox, and Ralph Malcolm. (1998, March). "Training Situation Analysis: Conducting a Needs Analysis for Teams and New Systems." *Performance Improvement, 37*(3), 18–21.

Langdon, Danny G. (1997, November-December). "Selecting Interventions." *Performance Improvement, 36*(10), 11–15.

Miller, Craig L. (1998, Spring). "Design, Implementation, and Evaluation of a University-Industry Multimedia Presentation." *Journal of Instruction Delivery Systems, 12*(2), 19–23.

Phillips, Jack J., and William J. Rothwell, editors. (1998). *Linking HRD Programs With Organizational Strategy.* Alexandria, VA: American Society for Training & Development.

Shank, Patti. (1998, August). "No R-E-S-P-E-C-T? Five Foolish Things Trainers Do." *Training & Development, 52*(8) 14–15.

CHAPTER 3

Austin, Mary. (1998). "Needs Assessment by Focus Group." *Info-Line,* issue no. 9401 (rev. edition). Alexandria, VA: American Society for Training & Development.

Brethower, Dale M. (1997, November-December). "Rapid Analysis: Matching Solutions to Changing Situations." *Performance Improvement, 36*(10), 16–21.

Gerson, Gigi, and Cathy McCleskey. (1998, July). "Numbers Help Make a Training Decision That Counts." *HRMagazine, 43*(8), 51–58.

Loughner, Pamela, and Leslie Moller. (1998). "The Use of Task Analysis Procedures by Instructional Designers." *Performance Improvement Quarterly, 11*(3), 79–100.

Ricks, Don M. (1997, August). "Challenging Assumptions That Block Learning." *Training, 34*(8), 56–62.

Russell, Susan. (1998). "Training and Learning Styles." *Info-Line,* issue no. 8804 (rev. edition). Alexandria, VA: American Society for Training & Development.

Tampson, Peggy. (1998, March-April). "Training Ties That Bind." *Technical Training, 9*(2) 10–14.

Waagen, Alice K. (1998, August). "Task Analysis." *Info-Line,* issue no. 9808. Alexandria, VA: American Society for Training & Development.

Zemke, Ron. (1998, March). "How to Do a Needs Assessment When You Think You Don't Have Time." *Training, 35*(3), 38–44.

CHAPTER 4

Cohen, Stephen L. (1998, August). "The Case for Custom Training." *Training & Development, 52*(8), 36–41.

Coombs, Steven J., and Ian D. Smith. (1998, May-June). "Designing a Self-Organized Conversational Learning Environment." *Educational Technology, 38*(3), 17–28.

Kules, Jack, and Mike Smith. (1997, April). "Produce It or Purchase It?" *Technical & Skills Training, 8*(3), 24–26.

Langdon, Danny. (1997, October). "Are Objectives Passe?" *Performance Improvement, 36*(9), 12–16.

Mager, Robert F. (1997). *Making Instruction Work: or Skillbloomers.* Atlanta: Center for Effective Performance.

Moallem, Mahnaz, and Rodney S. Earle. (1998, March-April). "Instructional Design Models and Teacher Thinking: Toward a New Conceptual Model for Research and Development." *Educational Technology, 38*(2), 5–22.

Parry, Scott. (1998, July-August). "Organizing a Lesson Plan By Objectives." *Technical Training, 9*(4), 8–9.

Plattner, Francis. (1997, December). "Instructional Objectives." *Info-Line,* issue no. 9712. Alexandria, VA: American Society for Training & Development.

CHAPTER 5

Gayeski, Diane M. (1998, April). "Out-of-the-Box Instructional Design." *Training & Development, 52*(4) 36–40.

Gordon, Jack, and Marc Hequet. (1997, March). "Live & in Person." *Training, 34*(3), 24–31.

Reigeluth, Charles M., and Kurt Squire. (1998, July-August). "Emerging Work on the New Paradigm of Instructional Theories." *Educational Technology, 48*(4), 41–47.

Ruyle, Kim E. (1998, May-June). "The 'Three Rs' of ROI." *Technical Training, 9*(3), 26–29.

Schriver, Rob, and Steve Giles. (1998, July-August). "Where Have All the $$$ Gone." *Technical Training, 9*(4), 22–25.

Siegel, Josh. (1997, September). "How to Combine Classroom Training and Technology Delivery." *Multimedia & Internet Training Newsletter, 4*(9), 4–5.

Webb, Wendy. (1997, February). "Multimedia Training on a Budget." *Training, 34*(2), A12–A18.

Yelon, Stephen, and Lorinda M. Sheppard. (1998, January). "Instant Lessons." *Performance Improvement, 37*(1), 15–20.

CHAPTER 6

Chinien, Chris, and France Boutin. (1994, March). "A Framework for Evaluating the Effectiveness of Instructional Materials." *Performance and Instruction, 33*(3), 15–18.

Dick, Walter, and Debby King. (1994, October). "Formative Evaluation in the Performance Context." *Performance and Instruction, 33*(9), 3–8.

Duncan, Jack. (1998, July-August). "WBT Simulations for Safety." *Technical Training, 9*(4), 32–34.

Northrup, Pamela Taylor. (1995, November-December). "Concurrent Formative Evaluation: Guidelines and Implications for Multimedia Designers." *Educational Technology, 35*(6), 24–31.

Provost, Kathy. (1997, November). "Implementing a Web-Based Training Project." *Multimedia & Internet Training Newsletter, 4*(11), 6–7.

Ramsey, Bonnie, and Pat Murphy. (1996, Summer). "Human Factors Considerations in Multimedia Courseware Development." *Journal of Interactive Instruction Development, 9*(1), 10–15.

Reynolds, Angus. (1995, November-December). "The Basics: Formative Evaluation." *Technical & Skills Training, 6*(8), 8–9.

CHAPTER 7

Bureau of National Affairs. (1998, June). "Evaluation Evolves." *Workforce Strategies, 16,* WS-31–WS-32.

Falletta, Salvatore V., and Wendy L. Combs. (1997, September). "Evaluating Technical Training: A Functional Approach." *Info-Line,* issue no. 9709. Alexandria, VA: American Society for Training & Development.

Hale, Judith. (1998, February). "Evaluation: It's Time to Go Beyond Levels, 1, 2, 3, and 4." *Performance Improvement, 37*(2).

Kidder, Pamela J., and Janice Z. Rouiller. (1997, Spring). "Evaluating the Success of a Large-Scale Training Effort." *National Productivity Review, 16*(2), 79–89.

Morrow, Charley C., M. Quintin Jarrett, and Melvin T. Rupinski, (1997, Spring). "An Investigation of the Effect and Economic Utility of Corporate-wide Training." *Personnel Psychology, 50*(1), 91–119.

Phillips, Jack J. (1997). *Handbook of Training Evaluation and Measurement Methods.* Houston: Gulf.

Piskurich, George M. (1997, September). "Reevaluating Evaluation." *Performance Improvement, 36*(8), 16–17.

Robinson, Dana Gaines, and James C. Robinson. (1997, revised edition). "Measuring Affective and Behavioral Change." *Info-Line,* issue no. 9110. Alexandria, VA: American Society for Training & Development.

Waagen, Alice K. (1997, May). "Essentials for Evaluation." *Info-Line,* issue no. 9705. Alexandria, VA: American Society for Training & Development.

Watson, Scott C. (1998, May). "Five Easy Pieces to Performance Measurement." *Training & Development, 52*(5), 44–48.

About the Author

Geri E. McArdle has been a successful human resource manager, educator, and consultant in both the public and private sectors. She was recently selected as the outstanding faculty member of the year in the Business Administration and Management Department at Johns Hopkins University.

McArdle was a fellow at the Philosophy of Education Research Center at Harvard University, and she completed a master's degree in teaching and technology at the Harvard Graduate School of Education. She has a PH.D. in educational and public administration from Syracuse University. McArdle has written several books and has been a consultant for many of the *Fortune 500* companies, including AT&T and the Xerox Corporation, as well as for the Department of State and the White House.